FIRE MAGIC

FIRE MAGIC

BARRY DAVIES

BLOOMSBURY

First published in Great Britain 1994
Bloomsbury Publishing Plc, 2 Soho Square, London W1V 5DE

PICTURE SOURCES

Associated Press: pages 3 and 6
Remaining pictures courtesy of Barry Davies
Maps and diagrams on pages 4, 5 and 7 by Neil Hyslop

A CIP catalogue record for this book is available from the British Library

ISBN 0 7475 1921 8

10 9 8 7 6 5 4 3 2 1

Typeset by Hewer Text Composition Services, Edinburgh
Printed by Clays Ltd, St Ives plc

This book is dedicated to the airline pilots of the world. But in particular, to those who have endured the terrors of hijacking. Especially Lufthansa pilot Jürgen Schumann who was murdered in Aden in 1977.

It is not the critic who counts, not the one who points out how the strong man stumbled or how the doer of deeds might have done better. The credit belongs to the man who is actually in the arena, whose face is marred with sweat and dust and blood, who strives valiantly; who knows the enthusiasms, the great devotions, and spends himself in a worthy cause; who, if he wins, knows the triumph of high achievement; and who, if he fails, at least fails while daring greatly, so that his place shall never be with those cold and timid souls who knew neither victory nor defeat.

CONTENTS

FOREWORD

When I joined the SAS the main criteria were fitness and a resourceful brain. But later I was required to pass Army education examinations, as I had left school with no formal qualifications. During an inactive year in my early days in the regiment, the Education Officer, known to all as 'Schooly', suggested that some of us try going back to college. We weren't too impressed with this idea since it would involve wasting good drinking time down at the pub. But this 'Schooly' was a dedicated man, and within a year I had achieved decent grades in four O-Level subjects. The following year I attempted two A-Levels, sociology and economics, and again, somewhat to my surprise, I passed. At this stage I developed my passion for writing.

Unfortunately, it is not always possible to write about factual events that cover SAS operations. Understandably, the regimental 'Head shed' does not take kindly to it, unless you are a senior officer and beyond reprimand. To some extent I go along with this veiled silence, and I thought very hard about what I was going to write. To compromise, the hijack at Mogadishu only actually involved two SAS men and did not seriously effect British security, and I decided this should be a factual book. The German name for this operation was 'Fire Magic'.

I have been trying to publish this book for years, but being a good ex-SAS soldier I asked for official permission and the answer was always 'No'. Finally I thought that if I didn't do it now everyone would miss out on a brilliant story. I say 'story' because it reads like that, but what I recount here is all fact, not fiction. The telling of tales is something I love, and my eighteen years in the SAS have certainly given me some tales to talk about. For me there is a personal bonus, too, for as I write, my memories of old friends return and once more they become alive. A lot of my mates, all of them good men, fought and died in some remote land defending the basic principles of freedom and democracy.

The story of Lufthansa flight LH181 – the background of terrorism, together with my own personal account of what happened during the hijack and its aftermath – highlights one of the most courageous rescue operations of our times. From the outset I realised that this story must be written 'on the surface', telling it as it happened in an attempt to capture the emotions and intimacy of the drama.

This book is not intended to be a judgement, in either the legal or historical sense; it is my reconstruction of events. Help in preparing it has come from many sources, not least Ulrich Wegener, then commander of the West German anti-terrorist unit GSG9, who kindly sent me a book giving the inside story of his organisation. My thanks also go to Lord Callaghan, then Prime Minister, for having the courage to send Alastair Morrison and me to join our German colleagues.

No one writes a book completely by themselves – we all need a mentor, a critic, and in my case someone to check my grammar. Sarah Thomson carried out my research and made sure that no small detail was overlooked; she also put up with all my stories. Alastair Morrison, who at the time of the hijack was second-in-command of the SAS, shared this adventure with me. Before putting pen to paper I picked his brains – I was surprised at how many of the minor details I had forgotten. It is also thanks to Alastair that we managed to get so far into the operation.

Also my sincere thanks go to all at Bloomsbury Publishing, especially David Reynolds, who has made sure that the whole process ran smoothly and efficiently. Finally, a big thank you to the lady in my life, Yvonne, for believing in me.

1

SUMMONED TO NO. 10

Friday, 14 October 1977 was a fairly typical day for me and James Callaghan. Since the previous Monday I had been at Heathrow Airport with a ten-strong SAS anti-terrorist team, familiarising myself with the design and detailed functioning of a major international airport and the aircraft using it. Prime Minister James Callaghan was visiting a shoe factory in Norwich as part of a tour of successful areas of British industry. But that day was to end in far from typical fashion when I was rushed to an immediate high-level briefing at No. 10 Downing Street – the result would be a daring and dangerous mission to rescue a planeful of hostages in the heart of Africa.

As the manager showed the Prime Minister around the works, an agitated assistant interrupted with the startling news that the West German Chancellor, Herr Schmidt, was telephoning from Bonn and wished to speak to the Prime Minister urgently. In the privacy of one of the offices the two leaders talked.

Chancellor Schmidt's call was in connection with the previous day's hijacking of a Lufthansa plane. Some time earlier the seven heads of government know as the G7 had agreed, at a private discussion, that all steps should be taken, if necessary to include international co-operation, to put a stop to the current spate of aircraft hijackings by terrorists. The Chancellor had been informed of a British specialist group known as the SAS, whom everyone seemed to hold in very high regard and who possessed both Middle East specialist knowledge and state-of-the-art weaponry. As the Prime Minister listened, the Chancellor suggested that such specialised skills could be extremely useful in bringing the present hijack to a peaceful end. He then indicated, in great confidence, that Germany was considering making an assault on the aircraft, and asked if the SAS could help. Mr Callaghan told the Chancellor that it was feasible but that he would need time to consult.

At around 4.30pm I and my team of men arrived back at SAS headquarters in Hereford. From the look of the weather we were just in time, for fog was spreading dramatically across the whole country.

The enormous purpose-built hangar that houses the anti-terrorist squad was unmanned, so, after checking in all our equipment and vehicles, I ensured that all my crew were on call and then released them for the weekend. I made sure the crew room was locked, then collected my small bag of dirty washing and set off for home.

Home in those days was a beautiful little black and white cottage about twenty minutes' drive away, which I had purchased as a derelict shell and spent many happy hours improving. But no sooner had I arrived at the cottage than the telephone rang.

'Duty officer, operation room. You're on standby. Return to the hangar now – the team commander is waiting for you.'

'I'm on my way.' There was no point in asking what was happening – the thing to do was get my backside into camp as soon as possible. Jumping back into the car I drove rapidly back to barracks, thinking as I did so that it could not be a major incident or they would have set off the call-in alerters carried by all the team.

As I arrived at the main door to the hangar I found the team commander waiting. Quickly he outlined the picture. 'The Lufthansa aircraft that was hijacked yesterday, it looks like we might get involved. The German Chancellor, Helmut Schmidt, has been having frantic talks with Callaghan most of the day. It would seem that the Prime Minister is stuck up north in a shoe factory and can't return due to the weather. The Colonel is abroad, but the second-in-command is in London – we are to fly down and meet him at the Ministry of Defence.' The team commander seemed very pleased with this turn of events.

'What do they want us to do – any idea?' Still talking, I took my bag out of the car – full of dirty washing it may be, but I might need it.

'The only thing I know is that the hijacked aircraft is now stuck in Dubai, and that we may be required to help.' He turned towards the helicopter pad.

'Wait!' I had a suggestion to make. 'I think it would be a good idea to get some personnel back into the hangar in case we need to call in – it would make sense.'

'Duty officer already has it in hand. Now let's go.'

We swiftly made our way to the helipad where the pilot, expecting us, already had the rotors turning. He was not too confident about getting us to London in these foggy conditions, but he was determined to have a bloody good go. Fortunately he was able to rise above much of the dense fog and, utilising the navigational beacons along the route, we made our way to our destination.

Unfortunately Battersea Heliport had been closed because of the fog – but the pilot landed anyway. Since everything was shut down tight, we had no option but to climb over the Heliport gates and jump down to the street. Luckily, one of the first vehicles we saw was a police panda car. Jumping into the road, I flagged it down. At first I was not sure the officer was going to stop, but fortunately he did – though demanding to know what the hell was going on.

The pair of us were wearing what could only be described as very casual clothing and must have looked very suspect. Still clutching my bag of dirty washing, I told the police officer he had to take us to No. 10 Downing Street. It was hardly surprising that he was a little dubious about acceding to our request, but my manner, backed up by military ID cards, persuaded him to radio through to his control. They played it safe, telling the officer to give us a lift, see if we were genuine and, if not, to bring us back to the station! I often wonder if that policeman knew what he was getting us into . . .

Ten minutes later we pulled up in Downing Street and joined a group of senior military personnel assembled on the pavement. There was a swift, huddled briefing on the current situation concerning the German hijack and as far as I could make out Britain was now somehow involved. The truth was that no one really knew what was going on.

Among the group was one familiar face – Major Alastair Morrison, second-in-command of the SAS, who had been at the Special Forces Club in London when he received his call from the duty officer in Hereford. Major Morrison had been my old Squadron Commander a few years back and I knew him to be a really good officer. Before entering the heart of British security, we were further briefed to dispel some of the confusion surrounding the situation. It was made clear that Prime Minister Callaghan wished to give all possible assistance to achieve the release of the hostages. To this end, we were informed that a couple of politicians from Bonn had arrived, together with two members of an organisation barely known to us – GSG9, a special West German anti-terrorist group.

Swiftly we made our way into a massive building which formed part of the sprawling complex of government offices that make up the Ministry of Defence. It took me several minutes to realise where we were – the next moment I found myself taking a seat around a certain very famous table. Our meeting was to take place in the Cabinet Office itself. As the Prime Minister was still stuck up in East Anglia due to the deteriorating weather, it was to be chaired by the Permanent Under-Secretary for Defence. Also present were various ministers, heads of British security departments, Major Morrison, the team commander and myself.

It was quickly established that the hijacked plane's position was still, as reported by the media at noon, in Dubai. Dressed so casually, I must say I felt a trifle uneasy sitting in the presence of such distinguished figures. That was until I listened to the conversation; then it slowly began to dawn on me that none of those present, apart from Alastair Morrison, the team commander and I, had a clue about anti-hijack methods – but why should they? They were politicians. When the subject came up, all heads turned towards the team commander and me. Briefly the commander explained the techniques of assaulting an aircraft and what equipment was available to us. Then I enquired about how much we should tell the Germans about the special items of weaponry that we had developed, like the stun grenades. There was a sudden silence and I could clearly see the ignorance on their faces. I realised I would have to explain. As I talked, I watched, amused by the looks of astonishment on the faces of those present. It was refreshing to find that these men of power were listening to me. Then Major Morrison reported that there was an ex-SAS man currently in position in Dubai called David Bullied, working for the Palace Guard, a force that had been SAS-trained.

The outcome of the meeting was that we were to comply

with the Prime Minister's directives and render whatever assistance the Germans requested.

As it was then around 8pm and no one had eaten, it was agreed that we would continue our discussion with the German delegation over dinner. But since the team commander and I were not suitably dressed, we were obliged to eat ours in the pantry like lepers. No matter, it was an excellent meal that included smoked salmon, supplied by Trust House Forte and served up to us by a sergeant from the Guards division.

After dinner the 'unclean' were allowed into the impressive drawing-room at No. 10, where a short gentleman in a penguin suit approached me and asked if sir would like a drink. Sir did – a large gin and tonic if you please, my good man. That was a mistake. Two minutes later he reappeared with a glass that was closer in size to a bucket. I took a sip and nearly choked – it must have contained at least half a pint of neat gin, and I couldn't even taste the tonic. The man in the penguin suit gave me a feeble smile: he obviously didn't like riff-raff in his domain.

Clutching my bucket of gin with two hands, I was then introduced to the GSG9 captain, who I must admit looked as uncomfortable in these surroundings as I was. Sitting around the large decorative fireplace, we talked, and within minutes I realised how much in common the SAS anti-terrorist team had with the GSG9. Suddenly we were talking like two long-lost brothers discovering how each country had independently developed tactics and equipment so similar that it was uncanny. As this German and I revelled in our new discovery, almost everyone in the room had stopped their conversation and was listened in fascination as we discussed anti-terrorist techniques. The only thing the Germans had not developed at this stage were the stun grenades.

I explained about the need to allow assault teams a few vital seconds in which to close with the terrorists. Royal Enfield

Ordnance, at the request of the SAS, had experimented with various devices of which the most favourable seemed to be the stun grenade. The device, called a G60, produces loud noise (160 dB) combined with high light output (300,000 cd) but without any harmful fragmentation. When detonated it is capable of stunning anyone in close proximity for a period of three to five seconds, and it is one of the most useful items in the anti-terrorist armoury. The effect is not dissimilar to the flashing strobes in a disco, but a million times more effective.

I also discussed our recent training on aircraft interiors at Heathrow and the methods we would adopt when dealing with a hijack. As I talked, Major Morrison explained to the German Minister Rufus about the SAS's expert knowledge of and military influence in the Trucial States, of which Dubai is part. The offer of our newly developed grenades, together with Britain's expertise and professionalism, encouraged the Germans to ask us to accompany them back to their country and then to Dubai.

As I sat bathing in my gin and tonic, the request was discussed in a three-way conversation between Helmut Schmidt in Bonn, Prime Minister Callaghan in Norwich and ourselves in the drawing-room of No. 10. After the Chancellor's request earlier in the day for SAS assistance, the Prime Minister had carefully considered the political consequences of British troops involving themselves with a German problem. Now, decisively, Callaghan ordered the SAS into action to help save innocent lives.

2

THE BUTCHER'S BOY

I was born, just as the Second World War was coming to an end, in Wem in the beautiful countryside of north Shropshire. My arrival heralded no major landmarks in history other than that I was born on the cusp between Scorpio and Sagittarius – thus my life has always seemed to be guided and protected by some strange fate.

I came from a poor but very loving family, and all my early memories are happy ones. My fondest recollection is of being coerced downstairs by my two elder brothers, early one Christmas morning, to ask our parents if we could come down for our presents. Creeping down the stairs, I saw that the kitchen door was ajar and I could hear them talking. As I peeped round the corner, there was my mother sitting on my father's lap having a kiss and a cuddle. At that moment my father enquired in a very tender voice, 'Do you still love me?'

'I expect so,' replied my mother.

Totally embarrassed at this intimacy I quietly slipped back upstairs, much to my brothers' annoyance.

Our family became quite large, swelling to four sons and two daughters, which was not uncommon in rural communities such as ours. At fifteen I left school without achieving a single certificate in any subject. It was a good school, but no one had enthused me to aspire – except for one of the senior girls. So, having received my first sex lesson on the back playing-field, I left Madely secondary modern school, now renamed Charles Darwin, and went forth to seek my fortune. Actually, I went to work in a butcher's shop.

While Mrs Coleman served in the shop, Mr Coleman would instruct me on the finer points of gutting and dissection. While he demonstrated the skills of butchery to me he would tell me thrilling stories of his Army days, which for some reason all seemed to be wonderful adventures full of daring deeds. Looking back, I think that these stories were the seeds that, once planted, germinated in my mind and led to my becoming a soldier.

One bright Sunday morning, at the impressionable age of seventeen, I broached the subject of joining the Army with my father. It was met with a flat 'No' and, despite my pleading, I got no further. So I ran away and joined the Army anyway.

A few weeks later, having finished work at about two in the afternoon, I secretly visited the recruiting office in the nearest major town, Shrewsbury. After I had completed the written test the recruiting sergeant seemed most impressed, and informed me that my results might possibly get me into the Welsh Guards. I was easily taken in – later I discovered that he was a Welsh Guards recruiting sergeant, and received a bounty payment for every man he recruited. Still on a naïve high, I was told by the sergeant to report next day to Sir John Moore's barracks in Shrewsbury, where I would be given a thorough medical examination. If I passed, he said, there was no reason why I should not join the Army immediately.

At home that evening I played it very low-key, said nothing about going to the recruiting office, and went to bed early. Next morning, while the rest of the family were still asleep, I got up as normal – butchers start work early. On this occasion, however, I dressed in my best casual clothes and, robbing the bathroom of a few toiletries, made my way to Shrewsbury again.

At around 10am I was standing stark naked while a tall dark stranger in a white coat held my testicles and asked me to cough as he assessed my fitness for Her Majesty's service. The time came to measure my height. 'Five foot six,' called out the orderly assisting the doctor. I interrupted, informing the doctor that the recruiting sergeant had said I was to mention the minor fact that I was joining the Guards Division. 'Five foot eight,' shouted the doctor, and obediently the orderly adjusted his notes. I was really impressed by my first contact with the Army – not only had my testicles been groped copiously, but in the space of a few seconds I had grown two inches taller.

I returned to the recruiting office where, in an upstairs room, I raised my hand and was 'sworn in'. Things got better then – I was given £30, together with a one-way ticket to Pirbright barracks in Surrey. What a great place the Army is, I thought to myself as I journeyed down. And then I reached the guard room at Pirbright.

'Good afternoon, sir, I've come to join the Army.' I was cheery and light-hearted and spoke with a smile on my face. Unfortunately the face to which I was talking didn't think it was a good afternoon, not that day, or any other day.

'I'm not a fucking sir, I'm a fucking sergeant!' he bellowed at me from a distance of two inches, spraying my face with spittle. He then turned and bellowed at some poor little man in uniform, who was sitting in the guard room. Immediately the soldier shot to attention and his feet started to move at a funny speed, just like a cartoon character. Like a bolt out of hell he went flying past me as if chased by the devil himself. The sergeant turned his attention back to me: 'Follow him, c**t.'

Despite this confrontation I settled in rather well. Two days later, my mother found out where I was and I was asked whether I would like to stay or go home. I stayed, of course.

Army life suited me and I took to it like a natural. After sixteen weeks' basic training I finished up with the 1st Battalion Welsh Guards, who were at that time stationed in Germany.

What can I say about the Welsh Guards other than that they are a fine family regiment? With good mates and the chance to stand outside Buckingham Palace, what more could a man want? Lots.

I must confess that I was never very enthusiastic about parade ground soldiering and much preferred to put on my camouflage uniform and play real soldiers. My wish was granted when the regiment was posted to Aden for a year and I was transferred to the Reconnaissance Platoon. Army life was getting better.

Aden, at the south-western corner of the Arabian peninsula, was a Middle East port of some importance and had been under British control since 1839. In 1962 the Soviet Union supported internal strife in neighbouring Yemen, which led to the overthrow of the ruling Imam. Britain covertly supported the Imam, who was now operating out of Aden. The problem was that the Yemen laid territorial claims to Aden. This sort of situation leads to what governments like to call a confrontation. To soldiers confrontation is loosely translated as action.

My first taste of action came when the 'Recce' platoon was stationed up country close to a small Arab village called Al-Mella. Our assignment was to safeguard the Royal Engineers, who were constructing a road. Several times our camp at Al-Mella came under 'Adoo' (the Arabic word for enemy) fire, but most of it was stand-off stuff. That is to say they would sneak up on us, mostly at night, and from a range of three hundred metres blast away for all they were worth; we in turn would happily respond.

One day, while we were enjoying a rest day, I and some other members of the platoon were playing volleyball on the concrete pitch which also served as a helicopter landing pad. The game was interrupted by the unexpected arrival of a helicopter. Fate seemed to be playing a role again, for that chopper was to change my life. We stood watching idly as it landed, shielding our eyes from the dust cloud caused by the down draught. Finally the machine came to rest and two soldiers leaped down from the doorway.

I say soldiers, but these were different. At first it was difficult to define. They appeared like giants, though in fact they were normal size. They looked intensely professional, but were irregularly dressed. And above all they operated with an air of supreme confidence. Then came the second surprise. Both men reached into the chopper and between them pulled out the body of a dead Arab which they unceremoniously dragged to the nearby medical tent. Then they returned and repeated the exercise, producing a second body which they deposited on top of the first in a disordered heap.

By this time some of our senior officers had arrived at the medical tent. Normally they would expect to be saluted and deferred to, but there was something about the two strangers that demanded respect – there were no salutes, no handshakes, just plain instructions from the two extraordinary strangers. After a few moments they re-entered the helicopter and departed. That is when I first heard that magic word, SAS.

For the remainder of that day the conversation everywhere in our small camp was about our clandestine visitors. The myth was strong even then.

A month or so later, back in the permanent barracks of Little Aden, I read the customary orders for the following day. It seemed that volunteers were required for the SAS. I was already hooked, so next morning I visited the company office and applied. I then voluntarily put myself through a period of intensive physical training. It was hell, but I knew it was my destiny and to be good enough for the SAS I had to be hard and fit. When I was up country at Al-Mella I would shoulder my heavy rucksack, throw a GPMG around my neck and stagger like a man demented up and down the runway. Back in barracks, I would run the roads until I was ready to drop. The worst thing was, I heard nothing. All my enquiries were met with typical army responses: 'What the fuck do you want to join the SAS for? You don't stand a dog's chance of passing.'

Then one lunchtime, as I stood sweating in the cook-house queuing for my meal, the company clerk slid casually up behind me and whispered: 'You lucky bastard, you're booked on a flight to the UK tomorrow night.' I was off to try my luck at the SAS selection course in Hereford.

3

THE RIGOURS OF THE WELSH MOUNTAINS

SAS selection is hard, and that's a fact. I recently read in a Bloomsbury SAS book this definition of an ideal candidate. He 'should be intelligent, assertive, happy-go-lucky, self-sufficient, and neither extremely intro- nor extroverted. He should not be emotionally unstable but, rather, be a forthright individual who is hard to fool and not dependent on orders.' That is a good description of the typical SAS soldier that I served with. It's what makes the SAS so unique – they're a whole bunch of individuals, but with the capacity to act as one.

Actually 'selection' is a funny word to use. The verb 'select' means to pick out the best or most suitable, while the adjective means chosen for excellence. But nobody picks or chooses you – you have to earn your place; it's more a case of the individual selecting himself. In most cases any man who gets through the selection process gives up all previous rank held in his original regiment and reverts to being a trooper. He then has to work his way back up the promotion line. I like this idea – it gives everyone an even start.

Selection takes place mostly in the Brecon Beacons of South

Wales, which, although not a high range of mountains, can be treacherous. Exposed and battered by constant weather changes, soldiers are seldom far from death by hypothermia – indeed, many have suffered this slow death.

Luckily for me, because of the self-imposed training that I had subjected myself to in the hot and dusty conditions of Aden, my stamina and fitness had increased and this helped me tremendously in the early weeks of selection. Fitness and the ability to read a map are the two main elements that help to get the candidate successfully through to the final hurdle, test week.

Test week is the real bitch. The best advice here is to stuff as much food down your throat as possible, especially at breakfast, because as sure as eggs are eggs, if you want to make it through the week you have to have calories to burn. Then, just when you think you have made it, you come face to face with the endurance march. Nothing prepares you for this. With a rifle and rucksack weighing 25kg you are expected to walk 60km in twenty hours – the problem is that the route runs up and down the mountains.

I started out early on the day of my endurance march and made good time, maintaining a steady pace until the late afternoon when, feeling utterly exhausted, I stopped to brew some tea and force some food into my tortured body. After resting for about twenty minutes, I checked my map and set off once more, still with 25km to go. But my body had already been through hell and was refusing to co-operate – as I stood up, I threw up. So much for all those essential calories I needed to burn!

With flagging determination, I staggered on as the weather started to change. Thick fog was now drifting in, cutting visibility drastically as darkness fell. Midnight found me knee-deep in a bog, staggering around aimlessly. Visibility was now down to arm's length, and to top it all I had lost my compass. But fate was there with me, and instinctively I felt that I was groping my way in the right direction.

Moments later, I heard the unmistakable metallic clang of a mess tin. Shaking my head to clear my vision, I saw the small glow of a hexamine cooker – a fellow victim making a brew, I thought as I limped slowly and painfully towards its welcome light. Then there they were, three army trucks! I had made the final rendezvous and done it within the allocated time. Shattered and disoriented, I nevertheless knew at that moment that I would soon enter the ranks of the SAS.

Continuation training followed, which included all the necessary basic skills required to fit into an SAS squadron as a new member. In the late summer of 1966 I passed – not only did I pass, but I also won the tankard for best overall shot. The latter was presented to me at the same time as I received my beige beret with its famous winged dagger. I couldn't give a toss about the tankard – I had the beret, and it was a marvellous feeling!

Shortly afterwards I was posted to the Mountain Troop of 'G' Squadron, and within weeks I was back in Aden. Wearing that beige beret and those special wings on your shoulder made an immense difference – I felt like I was walking ten feet tall. No more boring duties such as watching the road-builders: all our operations were deep up-country stuff, and I loved it.

Eventually the situation in Aden got so bad that the British decided to pull out. Once this was announced, the rebels started attacking any British people they could find. One December morning in 1967, the town of Crater (so named because it sat in the base of an extinct volcano) went ballistic when the rebels killed almost every European man, woman and child that could be found. I was sitting in Ballycastle House, by Khormaksar airport, where the SAS operated from, when a helicopter landed. Seconds later the boss stuck his head around the door and said: 'Move! Move now!' This may have been my first year in the SAS, but I was rolling. At the bottom of my bed was my belt kit, complete with ammunition, water, the lot. Shouldering my rucksack and grabbing my L42 sniper rifle, I ran for the chopper. Outside a small group was assembling, from which the boss was making his selection. Taking one look at the L42 sniper rifle in my hand he ordered: 'On the chopper. All Crater is hostile – Jock's got all the details. Go!'

The chopper took off and within minutes we were over Jebel Shamsan, the mountain that looked down over Crater. We let the noise of the chopper fade away, and then Jock gave us the full picture. It would seem that the rebels really were slaughtering all the Europeans, and our task was to shoot anyone or anything with a weapon – that included the local police, who had sided with the rebels. Our group of six members, all troopers, included three armed with sniper rifles; swiftly we made our way to a good defensive position overlooking the town.

Over the years I have become used to death, but in those days I was a novice, and I was totally unprepared for what I saw. The bodies had been laid out neatly in the street, deliberately allowing any traffic to run over them. I kept my cool – just. After we had arrived and started firing, nothing moved on the streets. A day later Lieutenant Colonel Mitchell, known as Mad Mitch, went against the advice of the High Commissioner and bravely led the boys of the Argyll and Sutherland Highlanders into Crater to retake the town.

Life in the SAS was full of minor skirmishes like that; your kit was always packed and you were always ready to go. And go meant anywhere – the jungles of South America, the frozen wastes of northern Norway, or the Oman war in the Middle East. I learned a lot and saw a lot in the succeeding ten years or so, and it all prepared me for that October day in 1977 when the lives of some ninety innocent people, at the mercy of a crazed, fanatical Palestinian terrorist, would depend on the skills, co-ordination and experience of a small group of German commandos and two SAS men.

4

THE BAD GUYS

From the late 1960s to the mid-1970s a group of terrorists known as the Baader-Meinhof gang were causing enormous problems to the West German government. During the seven years when this student-based, left-wing group were at their most aggressive twenty people were to die as a result of their activities, with scores more being injured. This may seem like a small toll of casualties compared with those of, say, the IRA. But while I deplore all terrorism, at least the IRA claim to be fighting for the freedom of their country from the British. The Baader-Meinhof, on the other hand, never seemed to have any justifiable cause for their terrorist activities other than their dislike of capitalism. They operated on a basis of pure destruction – terrorism for terrorism's sake. Their relatively small roll-call of victims resulted from the fact that they carefully targeted their victims, usually captains of industry and other representatives of established authority.

The gang had a small coterie of active principals, but also acquired quite a number of active sympathisers throughout Germany. These were people who provided financial assistance, safe houses and transport, and joined them on protest marches. During their most notorious periods the Baader-Meinhof also attracted a number of radical left-wing lawyers who defended their clients in court in a high-profile manner which attracted a lot of media attention. These lawyers took advantage of the complexities of the German legal system and frequently got their clients off on some technicality.

The gang was named after its two main leaders, Andreas Baader and Ulrike Meinhof, both educated people from comfortable middle-class backgrounds. Ulrike was a quiet, clever girl who studied German, philosophy, education and sociology at university. Here she acquired the reputation of being an intellectual and somewhat eccentric. But she developed into a self-assured peace activist who made speeches on student marches and in this way entered the political arena. From my research, it would appear that she then became a bright young journalist who was politically aware and became quite well known for her active social conscience. She had come to the media's attention after making several passionate documentaries which highlighted contemporary social injustices. She had also worked on the editorial team of the dissident newspaper *Kronet*, for which she had written an inflammatory article about one of Germany's better-known industrialists, comparing him to Hitler. The man sued the paper for libel, and the subsequent publicity made her a household name. This was to highlight her activities with the group even more, although she seems to have played only a minor part in their initial activities.

While Ulrike Meinhof was clearly motivated by a kind of idealism, Andreas Baader was driven by a more evil, unstable quirk in his character. From his teenage years her fellow terrorist leader had regularly broken the law, committing petty thefts and motoring offences. Some people have suggested that he suffered from a personality disorder. He was certainly given to long tirades of hatred which he would direct against whoever was near him.

Besides these two, the original Baader-Meinhof group included Gudrun Ensslin, daughter of a Protestant clergyman, and Holger Klaus Meins, the son of a wealthy Hamburg merchant. They were joined by Horst Mahler, a left-wing lawyer. In the early 1960s they had all been united in student protest marches against such universal issues as nuclear weapons and the Vietnam War. Like students everywhere they protested against the injustices of a capitalist society that seemed so unfair for those who could not earn enough to keep apace of the material demands.

The 1960s was a decade of revolution. All over the world youths were speaking out and the words of many pop songs of the time were a call to revolt. The Establishment began to feel very unstable and insecure – it is, after all, only a short distance from banner-waving on a student protest march to full-blown anarchy. People like the members of the Baader-Meinhof were at the extreme end of this surge of rebellion: urban terrorism was to become a new kind of warfare, and governments did not know how to deal with it. In 1977, indeed, the Baader-Meinhof would nearly bring down the Federal Republic of Germany.

All the books and articles that I have read would have us believe that the Baader-Meinhof group consisted of young people who felt it was time to hit back against their parents' generation, who they felt were smug and complacent. Personally I can find no real motive for their terrorism other than they were spoilt little bastards looking for thrills. The Baader-Meinhof claimed to have a convincing philosophy full of ideals which made them want to destroy the bourgeoisie and attack the capitalist system. They claimed that their political outlook was in tandem with that of George Habash and Wadi Haddad, leaders of the Popular Front for the Liberation of Palestine (PFLP). It's the old story over again – at least Habash and Haddad had good reasons for their activities, for they were trying to regain their homeland. In addition they were poor and dispossessed and had to fight for their education; they never had the security of comfortable middle-class backgrounds.

Nevertheless the two groups formed a relationship: German terrorists trained at guerrilla camps in the Middle East, and Baader-Meinhof and the PFLP would be linked in the 1977 Lufthansa hijacking in which I too would be involved. To give the impression of further international terrorist links, at a later stage in their activities the Baader-Meinhof changed their name to the Rote Armee Fraktion (Red Army Faction or RAF). This gave the public the impression that they were associated with organisations such as the Japanese Red Army or the Italian Red Brigades.

The Baader-Meinhof group first grabbed the public's attention in a big way on 14 May 1970, when they sprang Andreas Baader from prison. This assault involved a dramatic shoot-out resulting in the near-death of an innocent bystander.

Baader was serving a sentence for 'arson endangering human life' and was being held in Tegel Prison in Berlin. It was not his first time in custody, but this time he was serving three years because he and Gudrun Ensslin had placed an incendiary bomb in a large department store in Frankfurt. At his trial he had admitted planting a bag containing a device in a cupboard in the store. He had been sentenced but, while appealing against his sentence, had been released on bail. Baader absconded, with no intention of going back to prison. During his time on the run he made many underground contacts and increased his followers and supplies of equipment such as firebombs and guns. Then he was rearrested as the result of one of his contacts, who was actually a member of West German counter-intelligence. A meeting was arranged with a man who would supposedly sell Baader some guns, but it was a trap and he was caught and taken back to Tegel Prison. But he would not be staying there for long.

Ulrike Meinhof had kept in contact with Baader while he was in prison. They decided that they should jointly write a book on the welfare of young people, and had a publisher lined up. Baader then requested permission from the prison authorities to meet Meinhof in the Library of the Social Institute in the suburb of Dahlem, for research purposes in connection with the book. The pair were accompanied by two prison officers, and also present were two library assistants.

A man called Georg Linke was working in his office across the hall from the reading room when two women called on him. He asked them to wait in the hall and returned to his office. The next moment he was disturbed by a lot of unexpected noise. He went out and saw two people, both wearing balaclava masks and holding guns. One of them pointed a gun at Linke and shot him in the stomach. In the ensuing confusion, which had been further aggravated by the release of tear gas, Andreas Baader made his escape with Ulrike Meinhof, Gudrun Ensslin, who was later identified as one of the people wearing a balaclava, and another unidentified man. Georg Linke almost died from his injuries.

The government pulled out all the stops to find the members of the Baader-Meinhof gang: road blocks were put up all over Germany and hundreds of suspected 'safe houses' were raided. Posters were put up declaring: 'Ulrike Meinhof – Attempted Murder – DM 10,000 Reward.' Since the heat had been turned on, the gang decided that it was time to leave Germany, and it was agreed that they should go to the Middle East. Haddad's PFLP had promised them aid and military training at one of their camps in Jordan. So sometime at the end of 1970 the main players of the Baader-Meinhof gang flew to Beirut from East Berlin. When they eventually reached Amman in Jordan they were warmly welcomed by the leaders of the PFLP military and taken to their headquarters. Here photographs of them were taken and all their personal details recorded. Years later the Israelis captured these headquarters and came into possession of all these files.

From what I know of Arab training camps they are usually located in the middle of the desert, surrounded by high mountains. If not, they are very well concealed. A camp will have various flat-roofed buildings including accommodation for the instructors while the rest live in tents. Normally eating takes place in a simple cook-house which also serves as a meeting area during any free time. Close by will be a designated area for training and shooting ranges. These camps are rarely fenced, and would bear no resemblance to a Western military barracks – they are extremely inhospitable, rough-and-ready places. But training is not about smart barracks with marvellous messes and parade grounds; it's about the transmission of knowledge, in this case information concerning high explosives weaponry, hijacking and all the military arts that cause death. Despite the conditions, some of the Russian and Chinese instructors teaching in these camps would match any of their counterparts in the West. Vetting and security within the various Palestinian organisations are also very strict and rigorous. To put it simply, these camps are not for the faint-hearted.

At just such a camp the Baader-Meinhof group would have been fully trained in guerrilla tactics. However, according to some accounts the Germans, especially Baader, were not very popular with the training staff – in fact it seems that the Palestinians found them nothing but trouble. They were supposed to have separate accommodation, but Gudrun and Andreas insisted on sleeping together. Also, both Gudrun and Ulrike sunbathed naked on the flat roofs of the buildings in full view of the Arabs, who were not used to this display of female flesh. No doubt the Palestinians were glad to see them return to Berlin.

Once back in Germany, the Baader-Meinhof gang regrouped and prepared for a major onslaught against the government and capitalism. Ulrike Meinhof now devoted less time to writing and more to criminal activities, but had much less influence with the rest of the group than the media made out. The person with the greatest influence over the somewhat unbalanced Baader was Gudrun Ensslin, mainly due to the fact that they were still having an affair. Ulrike did, however, find time to produce a Baader-Meinhof manifesto entitled *The Urban Guerrilla Concept*, with a Kalashnikov machine gun on the cover. They were now calling themselves the Red Army Faction.

The gang's increased criminal activities consisted of fire-bombing, bank robberies and a nice little sideline in stealing cars. In the early 1970s they carried out several raids on various banks in their part of Berlin. They used illegal firearms to hold up bank staff and stolen cars for their getaways. During these raids some of the bank guards were shot and killed. By now the hunt for the members of the gang seemed to be developing into a kind of hysteria, and had become the main topic in the media and in domestic politics.

At the end of 1971 the group were hit by misfortune when a parcel addressed to them was opened by postal staff because it was coming apart in the post office. The package was found to contain sixteen pistols, three automatic rifles, silencers, telescopic sights, a large quantity of ammunition, 8lb of explosives and some walkie-talkie radios. Clearly the group meant business, and the government feared a renewed wave of violence and killings. Three thousand extra police were drafted in and a massive search of all known addresses was launched. Although these measures achieved nothing of major significance, they did reduce the number of safe houses and forced the gang to keep on the move, which curtailed their criminal activities to some degree.

During the next few years the gang continued to make successful bank raids in order to keep themselves funded. They also carried out further firebomb attacks on large German corporations and institutions, and attacked naval and army bases, always with the intention of maiming and killing. The newspapers published provocative articles stating that the Red Army Faction had declared war on Germany. In return the group wrote letters to the papers, declaring their avowed intention to cause major disruption to German society. All over the country members of the public were reporting that they knew where the gang were hiding. The police followed up these reports, but they were mostly wild goose chases.

Then one day in Frankfurt the police were given yet another tip-off, from a man who thought that a nearby garage was being used to make bombs. The police set up surveillance. On 1 June 1972 three men arrived at the garage; they were Andreas Baader, Holger Meins and another gang member named Jan-Karl Raspe. Immediately the police approached the garage but they were spotted by Raspe, who fired at them and ran off. However, the police managed to catch him.

When the other two looked out of the garage doors they saw the police coming towards them. Gesturing with his machine gun, one of the officers ordered Baader and Meins back inside. Then another policeman drove his car against the garage doors to secure them fast. Baader started to fire at the door, but his shots were blind and no one was hit. So the two of them remained trapped until police reinforcements arrived, at which point the garage was totally surrounded by 150 officers all pointing guns at the besieged men.

Despite the futility of the situation, Baader and Meins refused to surrender; they continued to smoke cigarettes and wave their guns at the police through the window. About an hour later the police decided to throw in containers of tear gas through holes in the rear of the building. Thinking that this would finish the two terrorists, the police announced through loudspeakers that they should throw out their guns and surrender. Slowly the two pushed on one of the garage doors obstructed by the police car as if they were going to do as they had been instructed, but it appeared that they found it difficult to move the doors because of the weight of the vehicle. Eventually the police shifted the car, whereupon the door opened wider and Baader laughingly threw out the tear gas canisters, forcing the police to back off.

Then the police sent for an armoured car with four officers. The two men were given one last chance to surrender, but they refused. The police then stormed the front of the garge, using the armoured vehicle as a battering ram. At the same time they threw more tear gas cylinders at the garage. But the armoured car was unable to get through the garage doors – in fact it just forced them shut more tightly, which meant that the tear gas containers did not go into the garage but started choking the police, who were forced to move back. At the same time Baader and Meins fired their weapons from the garage. What a farce – the SAS certainly don't do things that way!

Whilst all this chaos was going on, a policeman armed with a rifle equipped with a telescopic sight had gone up to the third floor of the building opposite, which gave him an excellent view of the garage and the surrounding yard. He took aim and fired at Baader who, hit in the thigh, fell screaming to the ground. Holger Meins then gave himself up and the police took their three captives into custody.

Two weeks later, acting on yet another tip-off, they found Ulrike Meinhof hiding in the apartment of a friend. During the previous fifteen days they had also managed to apprehend Gudrun Ensslin and Brigitte Monhaupt. At long last the German security departments must have begun to show signs of relief as they appeared to be getting on top of the situation.

All the prisoners were confined to isolation cells in separate prisons. On 5 October 1974, nearly two and a half years after their arrests, all except Monhaupt were indicted for five murders and taken to Stammheim, a maximum-security prison. The trial would begin the following year. When it did start it was without Holger Meins, who had died during a hunger strike. The trial was to be held at the prison, in a specially constructed reinforced steel and concrete building. So tight was the security that the entire area was covered with steel netting and all aircraft were banned from flying over the prison.

The trial of Baader, Meinhof, Raspe and Ensslin was turned into a cross between soap opera and farce. The press reported and highlighted all the events in the court. Quite often the defendants made ludicrous claims and counter-claims concerning the judge and the prosecutors. Baader and Ensslin sat together, laughing and joking and ignoring the proceedings. Quite often Meinhof would stand up and recite long political lectures, after which she would be banned from attending the court. The defence lawyers were accused of corruption and forced to retire from the court. The authorities were accused of denying the prisoners their human rights.

By the time they had spent four years in prison, most of it in solitary confinement, Meinhof christened it the 'dead section'. On Saturday, 8 May 1976 she was in her cell on the seventh floor where she could be heard using her typewriter. At 7.30 the following morning two officers unlocked her cell door. In front of them, hanging from the cell window grating, was Ulrike's body. It seems that she had hanged herself, using a rope made from a torn-up towel which she had tied through the cross-bar of her cell window. The prison officers called the prison doctor, who certified that she was dead. They cut her body free at 10.30am. During that time many officers visited her cell to check for clues and take photographs. An official post mortem was carried out and declared the cause of death to be suicide by strangulation. Oddly, there was no suicide note to endorse these findings. It seems strange that someone who had filled her life with the written word had nothing to put in writing at this final moment.

But whatever the events surrounding Ulrike Meinhof's death, Stammheim still housed three of her fellow terrorists. It would continue to do so until their role in the 1977 Lufthansa hijacking was played out.

5

KIDNAPPING OF A FAT CAT

Almost all the Baader-Meinhof's targets were male, and members of the industrial might from which West Germany drew her strength. However, they were very selective in their targeting, leaving the general public to walk fairly free and concentrating on what they call the 'fat cats' of Germany. Dr Juergen Ponto, head of the Dresdner Bank, the second largest in the country, was assassinated on 30 July 1977 when terrorists bluffed their way into his heavily guarded home and shot him in the head. His memorial service was well attended. Most of those present were heads of industry and commerce; among them was Hans-Martin Schleyer, a director of Mercedes-Benz and head of the West German equivalent of the CBI, the Confederation of British Industries. At the service Schleyer is reported to have said, 'The next victim of terrorism is almost certainly standing in this room now.' He was perhaps more accurate in his prophecy than he would have wished, for he was to be the next 'fat cat' victim of the Red Army Faction's loathing of 'bloated plutocrats'.

On 25 July a young blond man in his mid-twenties had approached a Cologne car dealer and after some negotiation purchased a white VW bus, registration K-C 3849. The young man gave his name as Peter Borke, with an address in Cologne: Luxemburgerstrasse 521.

On 30 July Arnold Last, an electrical engineer, had his yellow 300D Mercedes stolen from outside his house in the Cologne suburb of Porz. He was extremely annoyed, as it was a new car and he had just equipped it with a tow-bar.

On 3 August the caretaker of a block of flats in Wienerweg, Friedrich Wilk, returned from holiday and started to check up on the residents. In the basement car park he discovered a car previously unknown to him, a new yellow Mercedes 300D, complete with tow-bar, occupying a space not allocated to it. He blocked the car in with his own, so that it could not be moved. That evening two young men arrived, announced that they owned the Mercedes, and asked the caretaker to remove his car. When Wilk enquired who they were, one of them replied that he was the fiancé of a new resident, of whose arrival the caretaker was unaware since he had been on holiday.

Two days later, on 5 September, Wilk again inspected the basement garage. Again he saw the yellow Mercedes and, side by side, a white VW minibus and a blue pram. Thinking that the minibus belonged to a young couple in the apartment block, he scribbled down the number. It was K-C 3849.

At 5.25pm on Monday, 5 September a Mercedes car, registration KVN 345, turned into Vincenzstrasse. In the back seat sat Hans-Martin Schleyer. He was graded Security Risk 1, which demanded police protection. Following closely in an unmarked car were three bodyguards: Reinhold Brandle, Roland Pieler and Helmut Ulmer.

As they turned the corner, Schleyer's chauffeur stamped heavily on the brakes, stopping so quickly that his bodyguards' car crashed into the rear of the Mercedes. The reason for his sudden action was a blue pram standing in the road. A car coming in the opposite direction had made it impossible for him to swerve round the pram.

As the vehicles came to a screeching halt, five masked figures raced forwards and sprayed automatic fire at the Mercedes and its escort. The police bodyguard had very little time in which to respond to the machine gun fire now ferociously flaying them, though two of the men did manage to return a few rounds of machine gun and pistol fire before being hit. The chauffeur attempted to get out of the car and assist Schleyer, but he was shot by the terrorists. Within seconds four men had collapsed spattered with blood and Schleyer was being dragged, struggling, into a white VW minibus waiting close by.

It is obvious to me that this operation was highly professional in both timing and accuracy. Police estimate that during the ninety seconds of the attack the terrorists fired approximately a hundred rounds of ammunition, most of which hit the police bodyguards. The car carrying the bodyguards was raked with sub-machine gun fire, and all those inside were hit numerous times in the head and shoulders. From a range of less than four yards, Schleyer's driver had been carefully shot through the heart. The plan did not require Schleyer to be harmed in any way. Such attention to detail can only characterise the operation as being very professional – considerably more professional than the bodyguards. From experience I know that just a few basic tactics could have made a huge difference to the outcome of the kidnapping. What about putting the escort car at the front to cover any possible ambush? What about clearing the route? What about having the driver trained for just such an emergency? Why was the same route always used and the timings never altered? All these things go to make life very easy for terrorists, and whoever was in charge of those bodyguards would seem to have made some grave sins of omission.

Minutes after the shooting, following a telephone call from

an eye witness, two police cars arrived at the scene to find Schleyer's chauffeur and the three police bodyguards dead. Another witness, driving a BMW, had given chase to the minibus but lost it in heavy traffic. However, he managed to note the number, K-C 3849, which he reported to the police.

That evening West German Radio broadcast the first account of the kidnapping of Hans-Martin Schleyer. At 7pm there was a television news-flash of the attack. A large contingent of police were stationed at Schleyer's home and a tap put on his phone to intercept any incoming blackmail calls.

As all this information was being relayed the caretaker of the apartment block in Wienerweg remembered the white VW minibus and the blue pram in his basement garage. Friedrich Wilk quickly went and informed the police, who arrived around 8pm. In the garage they found the minibus parked in its original spot. Fearing that it might be booby-trapped, they brought in an explosives expert who opened the door with a piece of cable. Inside, the police found a photocopied letter from the terrorists. It demanded that the government call off all official search measures or they would immediately shoot Hans-Martin Schleyer. The letter was signed: Commando Siegfried Hausner, Red Army Faction.

In Bonn Helmut Schmidt, the Chancellor, had been informed of the attack at around 6pm. He straightaway set up a crisis cabinet and appointed himself leader, a role which he did not abandon for seven weeks. One of his first tasks was to make a television statement, in which he addressed the terrorists' question directly: 'While I am speaking, no doubt the criminals are listening in. They may be exercising the feeling of power and triumph, but they should not be deceived. Terrorism has no chance in the long run, for against terrorism stands the will of the state of the whole people.'

Late in the afternoon of the following day, 6 September, the Protestant Dean of Wiesbaden received a letter addressed 'To the Federal Government'. It is believed that he also received a telephone call from a stranger telling him to 'pass it on'. He immediately phoned the police, who collected the letter. Inside were two photographs of Schleyer and a letter which detailed the kidnappers' demands:

1. The release of the Red Army Faction members held in German jails: Andreas Baader, Gudrun Ensslin, Jan-Karl Raspe, Verena Becker, Werner Hoppe, Karl-Heinz Dellwo, Hanna Krabbe, Bernard Rossner, Ingrid Schubert and Irmgard Moller. These people were to be freed and allowed to go to a country of their choice.

2. The prisoners were to be taken to Frankfurt Airport at 10am on Wednesday morning and each prisoner was to be given DM100,000.

3. As some sort of guarantee the kidnappers should be accompanied by a Swiss lawyer named Payot, who was General Secretary of the International Federation of Human Rights.

Once again, the letter was signed by the Siegfried Hausner Commando of the Red Army Faction. A note from Schleyer himself was also enclosed. His part as a pawn in the subsequent hijacking of LH181 had just begun.

6

RED ALERT IN GERMANY

Looking through the British and German newspapers which covered the events at that time, it is amazing what a tight hold the Baader-Meinhof exerted on the West German government. News photographs of armoured tanks protecting the Chancellery in Bonn and of prominent political leaders under armed guard bring the situation vividly to life again. Yet I don't think that the terrorists had the collective intelligence or the co-ordinated information to make them aware of their strength. This was obviously the only saving grace for the authorities. However, I cannot understand the German government's reaction. Why should the kidnapping of one man invoke new laws? Why should this one incident cause all other major government issues of the day to be put aside?

After the initial shock had worn off the country turned itself into an armed camp. Most government buildings were protected with hastily constructed fortifications of sandbags and reels of barbed wire. Senior ministers and industrialists requested bodyguards and bullet-proof cars. At all German borderposts, guards with machine guns stopped and searched thousands of cars. Road blocks were set up and identity checks became a matter of routine. The government enacted new laws in record time so that they could deal with each new ploy that the terrorists dreamed up, but were subsequently accused of infringing civil rights. Squads of police and GSG9 – the equivalent of the SAS – were searching the apartments of high-profile left-wing figures without any justifiable reason, and these people were attracting media attention and public sympathy.

West Germany seemed to be teetering between a revolution on the one hand and a police state on the other, but Germany of all countries needed to avoid anything remotely like a police state which would only feed the insecurities of the older generation who had known life under the Nazis. In addition, at this time West Germany was once again becoming a powerful force in Europe. Its economy was strengthening while those of countries such as France and Britain were weakening. Bonn's clout in Europe was growing, and it desired the leadership of the European Community, then a purely economic union. The activities of the Baader-Meinhof group in general and the kidnapping of Hans-Martin Schleyer in particular were putting all this in jeopardy.

The kidnappers themselves expected and quite often got access to the national television network. They seemed to make fools of the Federal Criminal Investigation Office and also of Berlin counter-intelligence units. Eventually the authorities imposed a complete blackout on all news concerning the kidnapping, and what little news filtered through came via the foreign media.

In the early stages of the kidnapping the government crisis team decided to use delaying tactics, using whatever means available to them. The first tactic was to publish as little as possible, releasing only a fraction of the information that the kidnappers wanted published. Secondly, they introduced a go-between to negotiate on their behalf with the terrorists: Dennis Payot, a Geneva-based lawyer. Payot had been mentioned by the terrorists in their demand letter, was President of the Swiss League of Human Rights, and had defended members of the Palestinian terrorist factions in the Near East. There was no doubt that he had connections with the German group.

And so with an uneasy mixture of repressive measures and protracted negotiation the West German government tried to deal with the crisis on a day-to-day basis. On 5 September the Baader-Meinhof prisoners at Stammheim heard the news of the kidnapping on their radios. At 8pm their radios and television sets were confiscated, their cells thoroughly searched and all electrical items removed. A few members of the group were moved on to another floor or into new cells.

The evening news was dominated by Chancellor Schmidt, who said that the state must reply to the kidnappers' demands with the necessary toughness. The German people received the news with fear and alarm. The nature of the broadcast made the situation seem very dramatic, and solemn music was played on the radio for the rest of the evening. Herr Schmidt's closing words were that it was every individual's responsibility to 'provide all possible information to help capture the criminals'.

Herr Schmidt and his emergency committee which was formed to deal with the crisis discussed the demands of the kidnappers. Apart from those items already mentioned, they wanted a video transmitted on the late night news. This tape was not played due 'to technical difficulties' – this was probably the first stalling tactic and the beginning of the strict news blackout.

Dr Helmut Kohl, the leader of the opposition, claimed that France could put its terrorists on trial within forty-eight hours of the crime, and demanded to know why West Germany took years to reach that stage. He said that people failed to understand why defence counsel were not watched more carefully if it was true that they carried information between the terrorists. At Stammheim the

Baader-Meinhof members were now refused access to their lawyers.

By 9 September Chancellor Schmidt had cancelled all his political and other public engagements – a war of nerves was going on between the kidnappers and the government. For the moment the winner seemed to be the government, which had ignored many of the deadlines set by the group and had not agreed to their original choice of go-between. Various friends of Hans-Martin Schleyer were receiving letters from him written in captivity, pleading with them to help bring about his release. He had also written to his son, advising that the stalling tactics could not go on for ever. How right he was – soon enough the government's hand would be forced when other victims were put at risk.

On the 10th, Dennis Payot was accepted and appointed as mediator. Repeated demands for the text of the kidnappers' messages to be shown on TV were still being ignored. This control of information had deprived the terrorists of publicity and thus of their ability to put pressure on the government by frightening the public. As a result the gang decided to break through the blackout by contacting members of the foreign press.

A couple of days later various tapes and letters from the terrorists were deposited at different addresses. They contained proof of Schleyer's condition. An article in *The Times* on the 12th emphasised the hold which the terrorists had on the country:

> The result of the recent German government legislation and panic leaves it open to being isolated from the rest of Europe. If there is one thing West Germany needs now, it is a little bit of help from its friends. Without this there is a danger that its internal politics could drift gradually away from the central common ground which holds Europe together.

By the following day solidarity amongst the political parties was beginning to crumble. The Christian Socialists accused the government coalition of having contributed to the kidnap because they had refused the Christian Socialists' and Christian Democrats' proposals on tougher measures to combat terrorism. The prisoners were visited in Stammheim and asked where they would like to be flown to on their release. None of them appeared to know where they wanted to go, or even if they actually wanted to be released in this way. They seemed to be surprised by all this activity and were becoming apprehensive at various demands; Andreas Baader in particular appeared to feel that the government had few alternatives, and that one of the solutions to their dilemma would be to shoot the prisoners.

On the 14th an exchange of messages between the kidnappers and the eleven jailed terrorists was permitted. The contents of the message were not released, but it was assumed that the kidnappers were asking the prisoners which country they would like to be flown to as part of the ransom deal. Italian and French papers were sent recordings of Hans-Martin Schleyer because the German press were not able to print any of their messages. Someone representing the kidnappers phoned Schleyer's son and spoke to his mother, giving an ultimatum for her to pass on to the crisis committee.

On the night of the 14th/15th numerous apartments were searched all over Cologne. At one huge apartment building the police found a Mercedes car with the registration BM-A 812, which proved to be false. Inside they found the case from a sub-machine gun, later identified as being similar to those used at the scene of the kidnapping. Further investigation revealed a three-inch hole cut in the floor of the trunk, and a cuff-link. The cuff-link was shown to Schleyer's wife, who instantly recognised it as belonging to her husband.

Chancellor Schmidt now made his first official statement in the Bundestag, the Lower House of Parliament. He announced that the country would not bow down to threats and demands, and defended the government's decision to forbid both convicted terrorists and those awaiting trial for similar crimes to see their legal representatives until the Schleyer case was over. But he did reject the idea that for every innocent person shot by the terrorists a jailed terrorist should be shot in reprisal. This, he said, went far beyond the terms of the constitution.

Further discussions shortly took place between the intermediary Dennis Payot and the kidnappers concerning the destinations of the imprisoned terrorists. However, it seemed to appear that some of the countries selected by the prisoners were not keen on accepting them and providing refuge. The prisoners were apparently still able to communicate, albeit with greater difficulty; they were also able to hear radios in the cells beneath them.

On 18 September, the thirteenth day of the kidnapping crisis, there was still a total news blackout. The next day, in a leaked report, it was disclosed that an aide of Herr Schmidt had returned from a lightning visit to the Middle East in an attempt to resolve the situation. South Yemen, Sudan and Sweden were reported to have refused to accept any of the Red Army Faction.

At this stage even the foreign press seemed to have lost interest in the kidnapping – either that or they were following Germany's example of a news blackout. Whatever the cause, by now the kidnappers were getting impatient and demanding replies to their demands. As the government battled with the situation on the home front, Minister of State Wischnewski flew off to Algeria and Libya in an attempt to convince the kidnappers that the government were genuinely trying to find a country that would accept the prisoners. After returning from that mission he flew to another selected country, Vietnam, to exercise his diplomatic skills further.

A prison officer in Stammheim jail eavesdropped on the prisoners talking to each other through airways in their cell walls. The prisoners appeared to know quite a lot about what was going on. That day the cells were padded and fitted with chipboard sheets in an attempt to prevent any further communication between them.

At this point Jan-Karl Raspe asked for an interview. Since some of the countries that they had selected had refused them, he said, they had come up with some more choices. His use of 'they' suggested that they had communicated with each other to reach a unanimous agreement. He also complained about their being kept in isolation, and was apparently aware that a bill to keep jailed terrorists and suspects apart from their lawyers, and to restrict other contact with the outside world, during the course of terrorist kidnappings and similar crimes had been tabled in Parliament on 28 September.

On 29 September Minister of State Wischnewski flew back from Vietnam. On the 30th the Criminal Investigation Office sent yet another message to the kidnappers, stating that the Republic of Vietnam too had refused to accept the prisoners. That day's *Times* printed a poignant picture of Hans-Martin Schleyer holding a placard displaying a message in German which said: 'For 20 days a prisoner of the Red Army Group'.

The prisoners in Stammheim jail had now gone on a hunger strike in protest at the no contact rule. But because of the rule none of their relatives or the press on the outside knew about it. So the hunger strike was short-lived.

In France and Holland two members of the Baader-Meinhof gang were arrested for murder. But although certain investigations were coming to a head the kidnapping problem was no nearer to a satisfactory conclusion.

During conversations with the authorities and the prison

guards at Stammheim the main group – Baader, Ensslin and Raspe – talked about or inferred how they might die. The authorities concluded that Baader was frightened of being killed, at the same time suggesting that he might kill himself. Sometimes the suggestions were interpreted as a threat that he would make suicide look like murder.

I have read a lot about Andreas Baader, and the one thing that struck me about his personality was his attitude to authority. He had killed and wounded, robbed and committed arson, knowing that the worst the government could do to him was put him in jail. He also knew that as long as he stayed in jail his faithful followers would attempt to get him out. But the suggestion that he might kill himself is one that I find very difficult to comprehend. I can see the reasons for the German government to have assassinated him – it would be a very easy way out of a difficult situation. On the other hand, if he did commit suicide and make it look like murder, it would be a vengeful way out of a long-term incarceration – a final act of retaliation. But it was not his nature.

In *The Times* of Tuesday, 4 October Patrick Clough wrote from Bonn, summarising the current stage of the crisis:

> About 90 convicted and suspect terrorists are being held in complete isolation from the outside world under the new anti-terrorist law which came into force yesterday. They may not see or write to their lawyers, receive or send mail, have access to radio, television, newspapers or periodicals, or meet each other inside their prisons for a maximum of 30 days. The law, criticised by its few opponents as an infringement of human rights, was designed to cut off jailed terrorists from contact with the outside during the course of the terrorists' kidnappings and similar crimes. The authorities strongly suspect that such crimes may be organised by, or with the help of, terrorist

> leaders in prison – and that sympathetic lawyers act as go-betweens.
>
> The Germans believe that terrorists are also given privileged treatment in West German prisons. This, they say, helps the fight against terrorists as little as do the demands for the resumption of capital punishment. The Government is also urging quick punishment for terrorists, and that individual citizens clearly show that people do not understand why it could take years in West Germany to put suspect terrorists on trial, when in France rioters could be tried 48 hours after the event.
>
> French police are still searching for Herr Claus Croissant, one of the Baader-Meinhof trial defence lawyers, who crossed into France. When he is captured the West Germans want him extradited, but he has applied for political asylum. His Stuttgart offices were raided by police yesterday.

A few days later Lufthansa flight LH181 was flying over the Mediterranean, while the Bonn crisis committee was in session discussing the situation with regard to Hans-Martin Schleyer. There were numerous points on the agenda – the results of the wide-scale manhunt, security, justice and the media. Although the government had extended and managed to hold out against the kidnappers' deadlines, there was still no room for optimism. The crisis committee felt quite certain that if the demands weren't eventually met, Schleyer would be killed.

About an hour after the meeting ended, Chancellor Schmidt's telephone rang. Flight control in Aix-en-Provence had reported that flight LH181 had changed course and that it was a possible hijacking.

7

THE DARK-HAIRED ASSASSIN

If the reader should wonder why this section has been incorporated, it is because I believe that the man in charge of the hijacking of LH181 was responsible for committing the following murders in London prior to the hijack. Had the British authorities apprehended the perpetrator – and they had every opportunity to do so – the incident at Mogadishu might never have happened.

A Palestinian by the name of Zohair Akache came to the UK in the early seventies, apparently to study aviation engineering. Akache was one of the very few young Palestinians who managed to make his way out of the refugee camps. It is uncertain who funded his two-year stay in London or who paid his college fees – he lived in semi-squalor in a rented bed-sitter in the Earls Court area. Described as an intelligent, hard-working young man, Akache was something of a loner, although he did have a Yugoslavian girlfriend.

Like all Palestinians, Akache came under the scrutiny of British intelligence – particularly since he became very active in Free Palestinian rallies. In late 1974, on one of these occasions, he attacked a policeman in Trafalgar Square. He was arrested and identified as a PFLP activist, but charges were dropped and he was released with a warning.

However, in March 1976 Akache was again arrested at a rally and accused of assaulting the police, a charge on which he was found guilty. He was given a 'supervised departure'; this means that Special Branch officers escorted him to Heathrow and that, after his departure, the immigration authorities marked his file 'No Entry'.

But this ban made little or no difference to Akache. Using false passports he subsequently entered Britain on a number of occasions. The last time was on 23 March 1977, this time using a Kuwaiti passport. The security services knew of Akache's re-entry to Britain and the alias he was travelling under, yet no instructions were passed to Special Branch for his arrest.

His reason for entering became predominantly clear when, at 11am on Sunday, 10 April, the former Prime Minister of North Yemen, al-Qadi Abdulla al-Hajri, his wife and a Yemeni diplomat were shot dead outside the Bayswater Hotel in London.

The former Prime Minister, now deputy chief of North Yemen's Supreme Court, was in London for talks with Saudi government representatives and had taken the opportunity to bring his wife along as she was in need of medical treatment. He had been visiting the diplomat at the nearby Lancaster Hotel and both men had just got into an embassy car, which was waiting a few yards down Westbourne Street. As the car was about to move off, a man, described later by a witness as of Middle Eastern origin, moved across the street from where he had been standing on the pavement opposite the hotel, at the junction of Westbourne Street and Sussex Gardens.

The assassin opened the back nearside door and fired several times at the occupants with a silenced automatic pistol. Taken completely by surprise, the passengers could do little to defend themselves; in less than fifteen seconds all three were dead. The assassin ran off in the direction of Hyde Park and was last seen by Lancaster Gate underground station.

Police described the gunman as being in his early twenties and of athletic build, and approximately five foot ten in height. He was reported to be wearing dark-coloured jeans and a dark, three-quarter-length coat. The photo-fit picture issued a day later looked just like Zohair Akache. But despite the fact that the authorities were aware of Akache's presence in the UK, no attempt was made to stop him on his departure from Heathrow Airport some five hours after the shooting. Heathrow has an excellent security system, and the apprehension of Akache would have been simple had the security services informed Special Branch. In addition, an 'All Ports Alert' would have been implemented within minutes of the crime occurring. But Zohair Akache, who was in Britain illegally, boarded his plane for Baghdad a matter of hours after he was suspected of the assassination.

On 11 April 1974 *The Times* reported that a political assassin was being sought by Scotland Yard's anti-terrorist squad: details put out so far implied that this was a professional killing. Had Akache been stopped and detained, the hijack would never have taken place.

It was 6 October 1977, and in the holiday resort of Palma de Majorca another day of sunbathing and relaxation was coming to an end. The reddening sun dipped lower in the metallic blue sky as evening approached. Now was the time for the discos and night life to start. Already, eleven West German beauty queens were lined up for a group photograph in one of the more fashionable night spots – the fun and games were about to begin.

Later that same evening a dark-haired, athletic young man in his middle twenties entered the Saratoga Hotel in Palma and asked for a single room. The man had an Iranian passport in the name of Ali Hyderi. Regretfully, the receptionist informed the young man that the only accommodation not already booked was an expensive four-bed room. The Iranian took it without hesitation.

Next morning he approached the receptionist and again enquired if there were two single rooms available; again he was informed that the best the hotel could offer was a double. The young man informed the receptionist that a female friend of his would be arriving that evening and that he would take the double room. When she arrived she too produced an Iranian passport, in the name of Soraya Ansari.

Hotel staff described Soraya as being quite beautiful and in her early twenties, with a dark Mediterranean complexion and long, jet-black hair. Both are said to have acted like any normal holiday couple, spending a great deal of time away from the hotel.

Two days later a second couple arrived in Palma, both travelling under Iranian passports and giving their names as Riza Abbassi and Shahnaz Holoun. The couple occupied a room at the Costa del Azul Hotel, a short distance from the Saratoga.

After the hijack, the German investigating team in Palma revealed that these four people were very keen to fly to Frankfurt using Lufthansa. This information was confirmed, for although all four appeared to be on holiday, they nevertheless spent a great deal of time visiting travel agencies in Palma. Finally they succeeded in booking two first-class and two economy-class tickets on Lufthansa flight LH181, departing on 13 October.

The 'Iranian' Ali Hyderi had in fact been born in 1954 in a Palestinian refugee camp on the outskirts of Beirut, and he was a close associate of Wadi Haddad's. His real name was Zohair Youssef Akache and his parents had fled from Israel in 1948. During the hijack he called himself Mahmud and in his conversation with the pilot Jürgen Schumann on the flight deck of LH181 he admitted that he had assassinated the former North Yemeni Prime Minister some months previously.

8

A MAJOR WEAPON IN THE PALESTINIAN ARMOURY

The land of Israel was the birthplace of the Jews; it is their religious and spiritual homeland. Although exiled for 2,000 years, they have remained faithful to it in all the countries they have dispersed to. They had a right to return to Palestine.

At their birth, the United Nations foolishly planned to partition Palestine between both Jews and Arabs. But as the British army withdrew in 1948, the fighting started. Surrounded on all sides by hostile nations and with their backs to the sea, the Israelis fought. When they were not fighting they built, not just houses and schools but a nation never to be divided again. At the height of the initial fighting, the Israelis drove out many innocent non-Jewish families, often at the point of a gun; those that would not leave, were murdered.

> Our struggle has barely begun. The worst is yet to come. And it is right for Europe and America to be warned now that there will be no peace . . . The prospect of triggering a third world war doesn't bother us. The world has been using us and has forgotten us. It is time they realised that

> we exist. Whatever the price, we will continue the struggle. Without our consent, the other Arabs can do nothing. And we will never agree to a peaceful settlement. We are the joker in the pack.
>
> Dr George Habash, Leader,
> The Popular Front for the Liberation of Palestine (PFLP)

People do not just become terrorists, or hijackers – there is always a basic cornerstone on which all events turn, and in this case I think it was the foundation of Israel in 1948. A bitter internal war started and many Palestinian Arab families were forced to leave their homeland, now part of Israel, where they had lived for centuries. At the height of the fighting the Israelis drove out many families, often at the point of a gun; those that would not leave were murdered. Forced to live in refugee camps in miserable conditions, many Arabs wished to find some way of returning to Palestine. Among these were two young men called George Habash and Wadi Haddad.

George Habash, born in Lydda in Palestine in 1925, was the son of a wealthy grain merchant, and his family were practising Christians. Towards the end of the 1940s, like so many young hopefuls in the region, he was attending the American University in Beirut, training to be a doctor of medicine. In May 1948 he was twenty-three and nearly ready to leave university and set in motion his dream of setting up a clinic of his own. However, at that moment the occupying British troops withdrew and almost immediately the fighting started; within months his family were driven into exile. The Israelis took over completely, even to the point of changing the name of his birthplace. It was renamed Lod, and one day its major international airport would, ironically, be the scene of a major terrorist incident.

The memories of what George Habash saw and heard at those traumatic times were to affect him deeply. He finally graduated in the early 1950s and almost at once started a clinic for the poor in Amman, Jordan. One of the co-founders of the clinic, also a doctor, but a Greek Orthodox Palestinian, was called Wadi Haddad.

Wadi Haddad was the son of a teacher, born in Safad in Galilee. By the age of nine he too had become a refugee and was forced to lead a nomadic life with his family. The difference between the two men lay in their intellect: Habash was a brilliant student, whereas Haddad had struggled and qualified with difficulty. By profession and from their training both men were committed to the preservation of life. But the great trauma of their young lives haunted and embittered them. Driven by a crusading desire to liberate Palestine and let the world know about the Palestinians' misery, they were both to reverse their strongly held belief in the sanctity of life, and to learn to put death first. Some might see them as single-minded fanatics who would cast a shadow over the entire world.

In the years that followed, Habash discarded his religious beliefs and replaced them with Marxist concepts, exchanging his medical equipment for an arsenal of guns and creating the Popular Front for the Liberation of Palestine (PFLP). Although he continued to run his clinic for the poor, he was forced to move it from Amman to Damascus in Syria. Then, due to a change in political philosophy in the area, added to the fact that he had started to annoy the authorities, he was forced to move back to Beirut in Lebanon. In 1968 he was arrested and imprisoned by the Syrians for plotting to overthrow the government.

Wadi Haddad organised a daring plan to rescue his friend from a high-security prison. I wonder now, with hindsight, whether this was the precedent for the release of the Baader-Meinhof group. The plan succeeded, and the attendant drama reflected well on the newly formed PFLP. Its ranks swelled from five hundred militants to three and a half thousand active members, and won the support of many ordinary Palestinians.

George Habash spelt out the PFLP's policy in very simple terms. Its members were against the Jews and their re-establishing a Jewish state in Palestine, against Israel, and against imperialism. Habash warned that his battleground would ignore the borders and frontiers of the world and that his soldiers would go forth and create death and destruction without limitations. 'Our enemy is not Israel full stop,' he said. 'Israel is backed by imperialist forces.' After the PFLP had firebombed a Marks and Spencer store in London on 18 July 1969 Habash was quoted as saying: 'When we set fire to a store in London, those few flames are worth the burning down of two kibbutzim.'

Between them, George Habash and Wadi Haddad were responsible for the creation of the international alliance that carried the first campaigns of terror into Europe in the early 1970s. So effective were they that they found themselves under the scrutiny of Mossad, the Israeli intelligence agency, who tried several times to kill both men.

Habash was instrumental in setting up guerrilla organisations, with camps outside Amman which were to see the conception and birth of international terrorism. Here, fighters were trained in the use of small arms such as Kalashnikovs and taught the tactics of terrorism and guerrilla warfare. It was at the camp north of Amman that the entire Baader-Meinhof group were trained. Strong bonds were formed at these camps between Palestinian and European groups. Haddad went on to form his own PFLP Special Operations Group and maintained contacts with a number of international terrorist groups, including the Red Army Faction and the Italian Red Brigades. Haddad particularly respected the members of the Baader-Meinhof group and they were to become very important to him. He was responsible for such dramatic hostile acts as the multiple hijacking of three aircraft to Dawson's Field in Jordan in September 1970. That affair in turn led to the 'Black September' expulsion of the Palestinians from Jordan, and to the massacre of twenty-six people by the Japanese Red Army at Lod Airport in Israel.

The first of the Palestinian hijacks occurred during the summer of 1968 when an El-Al Boeing 707 flying from Rome to Tel Aviv was hijacked to Algiers. The Israeli passengers and crew were imprisoned for two months. In December of that year, another El-Al 707 was attacked. The sound of grenades and sub-machine gun fire was heard as it took off from Athens Airport. One passenger was killed, but the attackers were arrested. In February 1969 yet another El-Al 707 was machine-gunned when it was preparing to take off from Zurich for Tel Aviv. The co-pilot was killed and five of the passengers wounded. One of the attackers was killed on the plane by an Israeli guard, while the surviving three terrorists were sentenced to prison. But in both these incidents the imprisoned terrorists were released when further action was taken by the PFLP in later hijacks. The economic and social effects were obvious: airline passengers were becoming nervous and avoiding flying wherever possible.

In August 1969 the PFLP, led by an armed female terrorist, hijacked a TWA plane flying from Rome to Tel Aviv. The plane was taken to Damascus, where all the 213 passengers were released except for two Israelis. These men were eventually exchanged for two Syrian pilots held by Israel. The pilot's cabin in the TWA was then rigged with explosives and the plane destroyed.

It was a ploy that seemed to work well, representing both a threat and a bargaining chip. All these hijacks were to culminate in September 1970 with the Dawson's Field incident.

Leila Khaled was at this time an attractive, intelligent, dark-haired girl in her twenties. Her charisma had turned her into a folk legend, and the Palestinian and Arab youth idolised her. A former teacher in Kuwait, like Habash and

Haddad she was a graduate of the American University in Beirut. Leila had been just four years old when her family were driven out of Palestine. In an interview many years later she said: 'Like all Palestinians, education only helped me to realise what a loss Palestine was.'

Now a close confidante of Wadi Haddad's, she had become an important member of his guerrilla squads. In July 1970 she had been at his house, discussing plans, when suddenly there were several massive explosions, most of which seemed to hit the bedroom section of the house. After the initial shock, finding that they were both uninjured, they ran to what was left of the bedroom. Here they found Haddad's wife and eight-year-old son, both badly burned and disfigured. Mossad had just carried out a rocket attack on his home.

Khaled was to be the central pivot of a group which hijacked an Israeli Boeing 707 flying from Tel Aviv via Amsterdam to New York. The original plan was to send at least five terrorists to take the Boeing. Haddad had chosen Khaled as she had become a most accomplished hijacker, and for this reason she was keen to tackle the heavily guarded plane. He gave her the only copy of the navigation plans. All five terrorists were to meet at Amsterdam Airport. No one knew whether they had met before.

Unfortunately for the Palestinians, at Amsterdam suspicions had been alerted when three of the would-be hijackers, posing as passengers, insisted that their first-class seats should be near the front just by the pilot's cabin. The wary staff refused to let them board the plane. The terrorists, unnerved, failed to tell their other two collaborators, Khaled and Patrick Arguello, who were in another passenger lounge waiting to embark. As the final call was made over the tannoy, Khaled and Arguello made their way unknowing to the aircraft. They sat together on the plane, but did not speak or appear to recognise one another. Although they must have realised that they were now on their own, they were determined to carry on with the hijack.

Ten minutes after taking off, while the passengers were having their first drinks and beginning to relax, Khaled and Arguello leaped from their seats, shouted and threatened the 145 passengers and cabin staff. Khaled threw her hands in the air, exposing the two grenades that she was holding, while her companion gestured towards the frightened passengers with a .22 revolver. As Patrick Arguello made his way towards the captain's cabin, he ordered a stewardess to open the door. But he was intercepted and shot by a male steward who happened to be carrying a gun. As Leila Khaled made her way into the first-class lounge an unidentified young man, possibly a security guard, disarmed her. He grabbed her by the elbows and pushed her to the floor, then he tied her hands and feet together with string and a man's neck-tie.

The plan had failed due to the courage of the crew and captain, who now radioed a request to make an emergency landing at Heathrow. A full-scale police alert went into operation. Patrick Arguello died shortly before the plane landed. The steward who had attempted to restrain him had been shot three times in the stomach, but recovered in hospital in England.

At Heathrow the Israelis refused to hand over Khaled because they wanted to take her back for questioning and trial, but this was refused by the British government. Eventually the police persuaded the reluctant crew to hand her over. She was taken to West Drayton police station, where she was charged with entering Britain illegally. Leila was not particularly worried – she felt certain that Haddad would somehow obtain her release. She spent her time giving lectures on Marxism to the women police officers who had to accompany her everywhere. But even as this drama seemed to be coming to an end in England, another was unfolding in the skies over Europe.

On 6 September 1970 a TWA Boeing 707, carrying 145 passengers and ten crew, was flying from Frankfurt to New York. As it crossed the French coastline the crew were threatened and the pilot was forced to fly to the Middle East, where he was told to land at a rough desert airstrip in Jordan called Dawson's Field, which had come under the control of the PFLP guerrilla army.

Next, a Swissair DC8 flying from Zurich to New York, with 140 passengers and twelve crew, was hijacked over central France. Once again the pilot was threatened and told to alter his course and fly to Dawson's Field.

Then a Pan American 747 jumbo jet, en route from Amsterdam to New York, was commandeered by the PFLP. This plane had been hijacked by the three terrorists, who had failed in their attempt to go with Leila Khaled and Patrick Arguello. Again they made a mess of things. They could not force the pilot to take the aircraft to Dawson's Field because they did not have the ability to navigate it to this remote area – that was to have been Leila's job. So they ordered him to fly instead to Beirut, where he was allowed to refuel. The next day the hijackers ordered the pilot to fly with his 170 passengers to Cairo. There the hijackers, on Haddad's orders, wired the plane with incendiary grenades and explosives which went off just as everyone got clear of the plane, blowing it to smithereens.

Meanwhile, at Dawson's Field the PFLP held over three hundred hostages, consisting of crew and passengers. Without a ground power unit to supply electricity to run the air conditioning, the temperature inside the hijacked aircraft reached appalling levels. During the day the heat was intense, while at night it was freezing. The PFLP had rigged the planes with booby- traps and explosives, and although the Jordanian Army sent in fourteen helicopters full of troops, they could do little more than surround the airfield. A more aggressive stance might have resulted in hostile action by the guerrillas against their hostages. The PFLP made it clear that they would not release either the hostages or the planes until the release of Khaled and six other Palestinians imprisoned in West Germany and Switzerland. The three in Swiss jails were serving twelve-year sentences as a result of an abortive hijack on a 707 in 1969 at Zurich.

The British government was warned to consider carefully its treatment of Leila Khaled, who was still in custody there. To secure maximum publicity for their cause, the terrorists allowed journalists to conduct a press conference with the passengers at the now renamed Revolution Field. The passengers said that they were being well looked after by their captors and had food to eat; their biggest problems were stiffness and boredom.

Back in Britain Edward Heath, the newly elected Prime Minister, was in a quandary over what to do with Khaled. The following day a BOAC VC10 flying from Bahrain to Beirut with 115 passengers, 25 of them children, plus 10 crew was hijacked over the Persian Gulf. After refuelling at Beirut the plane joined the other two hijacked planes at Dawson's Field. The terrorists named the VC10 'Leila' and sent the passengers a crate of whisky to celebrate. Israel asked Britain for 'provisional arrest' of Khaled.

The British government seemed to be caught in a cruel dilemma between a powerful, immediate and obviously humanitarian call and a large, politically complex consideration. Heath was advised by the Attorney-General and Solicitor-General that, because the crime committed by Khaled had taken place in indefinable air space somewhere near Britain, perhaps over the North Sea and therefore not in British airspace, the authorities would have some difficulty proving a case against her. As the Heath government struggled for an answer, the PFLP reinforced the British government's anxiety by blowing up all three planes at Dawson's Field in front of the world's media. All the hostages were taken by the guerrillas and the Red Cross to hotels and houses in Amman and north Jordan. The hostages came from many different countries, so diplomatic relations were stretched in every direction. Representatives of the USA, Israel, West Germany, Switzerland and Great Britain met in Washington to discuss their options.

The Swiss quickly capitulated to the hijackers' demands. As they did so, the hijackers gave Britain an ultimatum that Leila Khaled was to be freed by 3am British Standard Time on Thursday, 10 September or the British hostages would be shot. When the hijackers blew up the VC10, Edward Heath decided that the safest course was to release Khaled.

She was taken to Ealing police station, which had been turned into an armed fortress with armed police at every entrance. The fear was not of her escaping but of someone trying to get in. A day or two later she was taken to board an RAF plane which flew her to Beirut. En route the plane stopped in Switzerland and Germany to pick up the six other terrorists who were part of the deal. The terrorists had achieved everything that they had requested, and the successful outcome was beyond their wildest expectations.

9

STRIKING BACK AT TERRORISM

On 5 September 1972, at the Munich Olympics in Germany, eight Palestinian terrorists forced their way into the quarters of the Israeli team in the Olympic village. Calling themselves Black September, a name signifying the PLO's defeat and withdrawal from Jordan in September 1970, they killed two Israelis and took nine others hostage. In a gun battle between the terrorists and the West German police nine of the Israeli athletes died, along with five of the terrorists.

The Israelis were horrified that such a thing could have happened to unarmed civilians, and swiftly took action. They set up search-and-destroy teams with names such as Wrath of God, which efficiently eliminated many of the Black September group, especially in Europe.

While the Israelis went and did their own thing, the lesson was not missed by other governments, including those of West Germany and Britain. Special units were ordered to be set up immediately. The basic international agreement on dealing with hijacking is reputed to have been one of the principal achievements of the secret G7 talks held just after the Munich massacre. Certainly all the anti-terrorist units seem to have been born at more or less the same time.

I remember the word going around the SAS camp. Six of

the boys were sent to the Rover factory and, with government sanction, took the next six white Range Rovers that came off the assembly line. At first the set-up was fairly uncomplicated, but as the problem grew and hijackings increased, so did the training and the professionalism.

The specialist teams were formed from existing military or police units. In West Germany the anti-terrorist unit was developed from the border police, Grenzschutzgruppe 9 (GSG9); similarly in France the Groupement d'Intervention de la Gendarmerie Nationale (GIGN) is also a police unit. In the USA, however, Delta Force was formed from Special Forces units, similar to the British SAS.

All anti-terrorist teams that I have been involved with are structured in more or less the same way. They are divided into assault groups and sniper groups, together with a smaller command and communication group. The strengths of each depend on the tasks required and/or the terrorist situation, but normally the smallest strength of any team is around fifty men.

Assault groups concentrate on methods of getting in, be it an aircraft, train or building. Snipers deal with any long-range situation that may present itself. Although the two groups exercise independently, a lot of cross-training goes on in order to create flexibility if the situation demands it.

All members of the SAS anti-terrorist team spend hundreds of hours in the famous 'Killing House', a flat-roofed block in the grounds of the Hereford base. This structure was designed and built with the express purpose of perfecting individual shooting skills in a large number of different circumstances. This highly sophisticated facility has been copied in both Germany and the USA.

Due to the high number of personnel practising at any one time and the amount of rounds fired daily, safety is of the utmost importance. Weapon training starts from the very basics of pistol work, and encompasses problems such as dealing with a moving target and weapon failure. It then progresses to more advanced techniques, using automatic weapons.

Here the famous SAS 'double tap' is learnt. This involves firing two shots in rapid succession from the Browning 9mm high-power pistol – two rounds stop a terrorist better than one. It took me several years to become comfortable with this method of shooting, but the technique has proved itself over and over again.

I have practised many shooting skills in the 'Killing House', and by far my favourite is the snatch. This is a drill which is practised as part of the hostage rescue scenario. The 'hostage' sits in absolute darkness, surrounded by silence. Abruptly, the door bursts open and a stun grenade explodes inches from them as laser beams of light penetrate the blackness, searching hungrily for targets. The SAS practise this manoeuvre on visiting VIP's, who at this stage do not move. It's not that they are doing as instructed, or fear that any movement might bring them into contact with the hail of bullets spitting within inches of their body – it's pure, unqualified fright. Luckily they are plucked up, albeit roughly, by black-clad figures and literally thrown out of the room, surprised later to discover not a single scratch upon their person. Out of respect for security I will refrain from naming any specific persons, but those VIPs who have visited Hereford and sat in the hot seat while live rounds smash into targets within inches of them will know what I mean – hey, Mrs T.?

All assault team members wear a black one-piece fire-retardant suit, on top of which goes their body armour and weaponry. This is normally a Heckler and Koch MP5 sub-machine gun that clips flush across the chest; there is in addition a low-slung Browning high-power pistol which is strapped to the leg for back-up or for use in confined spaces. Respirators are normally carried in a container strapped to the back, but more frequently the pack is discarded and the respirator is shoved up the left sleeve where it is available for immediate use. Most actions now involve wearing the respirator – it not only protects the wearer against gas, but it gives the black-clad attackers a terrifying, dehumanised anonymity.

Sniper's dress is frequently identical to that of the assault teams, but excellent camouflage clothing is also used. Again the same weaponry is issued, but in addition these men have two sniper rifles – one for daytime use and one fitted with a night scope. The main sniper weapon used when I was last on the team was a Finnish Tikka M55, but this has since been changed for the British Accuracy International PM sniper rifle.

An enormous amount of training goes into creating a skilful shot, whether in the assault or sniper role. I really enjoy shooting, and when I first joined the Army I shot competitively at Bisley – but that was nothing compared to the complex shooting demanded in a hostage situation. In conditions of absolute darkness and uncertain surroundings the SAS soldier must identify, confirm and act rapidly in order to shoot the enemy and miss his colleagues or innocent bystanders; this can only be achieved by constant and rigorous training in realistic conditions.

Specialist equipment can take years to perfect. The film taken of the Iranian Embassy siege shows a group of black-clad figures balancing precariously on the balcony attaching something to the window. Seconds later they slip a few feet to the side and the window opens with a thundering blast. In they jump, lobbing stun grenades before them. It wasn't always like that.

To cut a hole in a wall or take out a window frame requires a precise explosive cutting charge. The guidelines are simple – make a hole in the wall or window, but don't damage any hostages inside. In order to perfect this technique, in the early days the Ministry of Defence allowed the SAS to train on a number of old married quarters, most of them tucked away discreetly in some remote corner of a barracks or airfield.

During my sixteen-week demolitions course I learned all the technical formulas for applying just the right amount of explosive to cut steel or concrete. But above all I learned the basic SAS formula for estimating the correct amount if all else fails – it's called 'Add P for plenty.'

One day when we were assessing the amount of explosive needed to cut through a normal house wall, I strapped a frame charge to the side of a disused RAF house, then rigged the detonator to the 'shrike' (a device for setting off explosives, specially developed by the SAS). The idea was that we would carry out a practice house assault, entering through the hole in the wall that I was about to make. Poised safely around the corner, I set the charge off. 'Go, go, go!' I shouted.

Through the dust and the debris we charged forward, only to find no hole – in fact no house. Too much explosive, by the looks of it – back to the drawing board.

Many people believe that the SAS have a licence to kill, but in fact they are answerable to the law like everyone else. This is not necessarily so in other European countries. During any major terrorist incident in the UK Hereford is normally requested to stand by the chief constable of the relevant police force. Control of all terrorist incidents in Britain is firmly in the hands of the civilian authority. Only when the situation demands the use of immediate action to stop the further loss of life will the SAS act, and then only when command has been officially passed from the police to the military. Operations overseas depend totally on the country and the situation.

Anti-terrorist teams in most countries operate in the same way as far as equipment and tactics are concerned. It is only the type of personnel and the amount of training they receive that differentiates them. The major distinction between the

SAS and the GSG9, for instance, is that one is military and the other police.

That may not seem such a big difference, but it is. The SAS work on a rota system broken down into roughly five-month blocks. We would spend say five months in the Middle East or wherever the fighting is at the time, five months on the anti-terrorist team, five months on things I can't talk about and five months training on new techniques and equipment. Somwhere amid this rotation you find time for the odd occasion to get laid, or divorced. The point I am trying to make is that the SAS is always active, and its soldiers have a lot of real combat experience.

The German GSG9, on the other hand, only have their police duties. This arrangement does give them a good edge for dealing with domestic terrorist incidents. But until Mogadishu in the autumn of 1977, the GSG9 were untested. This was the first military operation outside Germany since the Second World War and they performed brilliantly.

The Israelis would have us believe that their anti-terrorist force is made up as and when they require it. It's not. They use a force called Sayaret Matkal (the Unit). True, this force does contain soldiers of very high calibre, most of whom come from the parachute regiments of the famous Golani Brigade. I have trained with them and they are a very impressive team. The unit was first formed after the Munich Olympic massacre, when they were known as the 'Wrath of God', or hit teams. Later they formed into the anti-terrorist unit that carried out the fantastic rescue at Entebbe. Now they are the strong arm of the Israeli Intelligence Service, the Mossad.

The American Delta Force was raised in 1977 by a man called Colonel Charles Beckwith, and he was some soldier. He had been attached to the SAS on exchange in 1962, and had served in Malaya. When he returned to the USA, the first thing he did was to write a report on raising a special unit based along the lines of the SAS. It then took Charlie until 1977 to get his plans for Delta passed by the Chiefs of Staff.

At last Charlie was given the old stockade (jail) in the Special Forces base at Fort Bragg, North Carolina. During the conversion of the stockade, the word Mogadishu suddenly hit the headlines. Slowly it emerged that a special German force, the GSG9, had attempted a rescue of a Lufthansa plane. What interested Charlie more was the fact that they had used SAS stun grenades. In the Pentagon the shit hit the fan, especially when the President asked, 'Do we have the same capability?'. From that moment on, Delta was assured of its future.

When Charlies Beckwith formed Delta he based his training as closely as possible to the SAS selection. Today there are very close ties between the American unit and the SAS, and on more than one occasion Delta have helped us out with specialist kit and equipment.

After the success of the Israelis at Entebbe and the Germans at Mogadishu the American Delta Force set out to free the hostages in Iran. Sadly they failed.

10

VICTORY AT ENTEBBE

After Dawson's Field, it was difficult to see how the West could counter airliner hijacking. When the hijack to Entebbe began, to the Israeli government the situation must have looked impossible. But unlike the rest of the world, the Israelis cannot afford the luxury of surrender – to do so could have spelt the end of their nation. So action was taken, and the resulting success was a direct challenge to all other nations to act with similar courage and conviction against hijackings. By 1977, as I was to discover from personal experience, the British and West German governments were not prepared to capitulate to threats.

Wilfred Boese was twenty-nine in 1976. A tall, good-looking West German, with fair hair and penetrating blue eyes, Boese was a lawyer by profession; but when he wasn't practising law he was a full-time member of the Baader-Meinhof gang. He was described as an intelligent man with a smooth, persuasive manner – a manner he used to coerce four other terrorists into hijacking a French aircraft.

At this time, most of the gang were under strict supervision in German jails. But in May 1976 Ulrike Meinhof was found hanging in her cell at Stammheim. Boese had always respected Meinhof, so in retaliation he began planning with the Palestinians for the hijacking of another airliner. The team consisted of two Palestinians from the PFLP and another Baader-Meinhof member, Gabrielle Tiedemann.

Tiedemann was a short, stocky woman in her early twenties, with short, dark hair, a round, podgy face and an abrasive manner. Like Boese, she had known Ulrike Meinhof well and the action they were to carry out was to be in Meinhof's name.

The group gathered in Kuwait to plan and train for the operation. They intended to make it the most spectacular hijacking ever; their target was an Air France airbus flying from Tel Aviv to Paris via Athens.

The whole affair was to be overseen by the master of hijackings, Dr Wadi Haddad, who would direct events from his operations base in Mogadishu, Somalia, on the east coast of Africa. Also playing a vital role was the President of Uganda, Idi Amin. Amin had already declared himself a sympathiser with the Palestinian movement and had welcomed PFLP training camps in Uganda. In exchange for this protection and the facilities of his country, the Ugandan President would be given the role of mediator. Such a role was irresistible to the megalomaniac Amin, who hoped that it would proclaim him as a prominent statesman to the rest of the world.

The scenario seemed foolproof. The team would fly from Kuwait and board the aircraft during its stop-over in Athens. Once airborne, they would hijack the plane and force it to fly south to Benghazi in Libya. After refuelling, and under the defensive shield of Libya, it would continue south to Entebbe. There the team would come under the protection of Idi Amin, with his twenty thousand-strong army. So confident were the hijackers of their success, and so cocksure were they that their demands would be met, that they deliberately proposed to extend the deadlines in order to get maximum media attention around the world.

In the early hours of 27 June, they left their apartment in

Kuwait and, travelling in pairs, drove to the airport. Here they boarded the scheduled flight for Athens. On arrival both groups went straight to the transfer lounge, which meant that they would not have to pass through security again.

As they boarded flight 139 for Paris, the aircraft was already carrying more than a hundred Israelis who had boarded at Tel Aviv. The two Germans had booked first-class tickets, while the two Palestinians were seated in economy. During the flight Boese went to the rear toilets, where he met up with one of the Palestinians and collected some weapons. He then returned to his seat next to Tiedemann and gave her a weapon. It would seem that the Germans had entered the aircraft cleanly, and the risk of carrying the weapons on board had been taken by the Palestinians.

Once the captain, Michel Bacos, had established his aircraft on the correct flight path, he handed over control to his co-pilot. Back in the cabin the crew of nine stewardesses started the mammoth task of serving drinks to the 258 passengers on board. Suddenly a young woman stood up in the aisle and raised her arms above her head. At first the stewardess thought she was stretching – then, to her horror, she realised that the girl was holding two grenades. The passengers started screaming. 'Sit down! Sit down! Everyone must sit down!' she commanded.

At the same time Wilfred Boese walked up the aisle waving a pistol and repeated the order for everyone to sit down. Walking past the girl, he made his way to the flight deck. Panic broke out in the tourist section, and screams and shouts could be heard coming from the passengers.

Then the two Palestinians stood up, brandishing weapons, and repeated Tiedemann's call for everyone to sit down and keep quiet. 'We are Palestinians,' they said. 'If you remain seated and do as you are told, no one will be harmed.' The message was repeated over and over, and slowly the turmoil subsided. Quickly the two Palestinians strapped boxes, which they told the passengers contained explosives, to the two emergency doors halfway down the aircraft. Then they warned the passengers that if anyone tried to do anything silly, they would blow up the plane.

Suddenly the intercom was switched on, and the frightened passengers listened as a man with a heavy German accent told them that they were being hijacked by members of the Che Guevara Commando Unit of the Popular Front for the Liberation of Palestine. He explained that the aircraft had been hijacked to convince Israel of the rights of the Palestinian people, and that the passengers would be held hostage for the release of many 'freedom fighters' presently in prison in Israel and Germany. He reiterated that the hijack team bore no animosity towards the hostages and that they would be in no danger providing they did exactly as they were told.

Back on the flight deck Boese made his instructions clear to Captain Bacos. The pilot in return assured him that he would fly wherever they were required to go and made it quite clear that his main concern was for the safety of the passengers. Boese's instructions were to take the airbus to Benghazi for refuelling, therefore enabling them afterwards to reach Entebbe.

In the early hours of the following morning the airbus brushed over Lake Victoria and touched down at Entebbe Airport. Boese made an announcement over the intercom, informing the passengers that they had now landed and that their ordeal was over. So convincing was he at this stage that many of the passengers began to clap and some cried for joy. Only later did it become obvious that the hijackers were not about to release anybody.

The moment it landed, the aircraft was ringed with Ugandan troops. To the passengers, however, this would seem a normal precaution in the event of a hijacking. A little later a service vehicle pulled up next to the plane and within minutes the stewardessess were dispensing cartons of drinks, a familiar procedure which put everyone in a relaxed mood. However, as the day progressed, so the heat inside the aircraft increased; no one had moved for several hours, and now many people became restless. Slowly the mistrust started to creep back. At last the 257 passengers were allowed to leave the aircraft, and under a tight cordon of Ugandan soldiers were forced into the old terminal building. Many of the passengers at first thought that the Ugandan soldiers were there to assist them, but it soon became obvious that the hijackers and the Ugandan soldiers were co-operating. As the dejected passengers realised the truth, many of them lost hope.

In the Israeli Parliament, the Knesset, an emergency session was under way. Prime Minister Yitzhak Rabin informed the members of his government about the hijack and told them that they could expect to receive demands from the hijackers fairly soon.

In the normal course of events things are fairly cut and dried: the hijackers take over an aircraft and then make their demands. However, in this case there was a major difference. Israeli radar had watched flight 139 as it had diverted from its normal flight path and headed towards Benghazi. Their first thought was that the hijackers must be Libyan, but later they had watched as the aircraft flew south to Entebbe.

There was no doubt in the minds of the Israelis that the hijack had been painstakingly planned, and now the hostages were being held in a hostile country. It was also obvious that the hijackers were being assisted by Idi Amin. Although the situation seemed impossible, the Defence Minister, Shimon Perez, and the General Chief of Staff, General Gur, immediately set their minds to working out a rescue plan. From the start they knew there would have to be a military option, even without the authority of the Knesset. If they capitulated, they knew that the damage to Israel would be frightful, and that the Palestinians would know they had at last found a weak spot in Israel's armour. As General Gur stated, 'It is better that we fail and our hostages die than we surrender to these people.'

First on the agenda was to alert Mossad, the eyes and ears of the Israeli nation, around the world. Secondly, General Gur issued orders for the recall of Israel's finest soldiers, known as 'The Unit'.

Assembling a strike force was one thing; the major problem lay in how to get them to Entebbe undetected, then rescue 270 people and get them home safely. The flight down could be worked out, given all the correct data. But once there, what resistance would they find from the Ugandan Army?

There was very little hope that the Israeli government could negotiate with Idi Amin, who by now had become totally preposterous. On the other hand, it was highly unlikely that he would dare kill 279 passengers of which many were from Western countries. Life in Uganda may have been cheap, but Idi Amin was not such an idiot as to expect the West to ignore such an atrocity.

At this stage a piece of luck came the Israelis' way: it would appear that an Israeli construction firm had built the new terminal building at Entebbe. Full reports, together with drawings of the old buildings, were shipped immediately to the Defence Room. Engineers who had actually worked on the project were tracked down. Just as all this information was amassed, a new problem arose: just a few hundred yards from the airport perimeter the Ugandan Army had a camp containing some two thousand troops.

Back in Entebbe, the hostages were still crowded in the old terminal building, a long, two-storey structure now derelict and falling into decay. Outside the building were Ugandan troops and the four hijackers, who from time to time disappeared for talks with Idi Amin. Throughout the night food and drink were supplied and, to start with at any rate, the toilets were usable.

Then Idi Amin, resplendent in a military uniform, arrived and to the surprise of the hostages informed them not to worry – that he was their father and that they would soon all be released. Adopting his favourite high-profile persona, he jovially boasted that he was negotiating with the Israeli government for their release. Ignoring his rhetoric, there was no doubt in the minds of the hostages that, had he so desired, Idi Amin could have used his soldiers to overcome the hijackers.

On Tuesday, 29 June, Wilfred Boese announced that because of the crowding they intended to move some of the hostages to another room. This seemed like a good idea until the list of names was called out: all were either Israeli or Jewish-sounding. Some of the Israeli hostages then plucked up their courage and shouted at Boese and Tiedemann that they were nothing less than Nazis. Boese was quite taken aback, and tried to explain that there was nothing sinister about the proposal.

The following day, as if to support his claim, forty-seven passengers from among the non-Israelis were taken out and flown to Paris. Again Idi Amin arrived to let the rest know that he had sent some of them home, although he neglected to say that none were Israelis.

Meanwhile, plans for rescuing the hostages were well advanced, but it would seem that the more they planned the more problems arose. Even though the number of hostages had been reduced, some two hundred people remained in Entebbe to be rescued and several aircraft would be needed. Under horrendous pressure, the Israeli Cabinet decided to release some of the Palestinian hostages. This decision was cabled via Paris to the Somali ambassador in Kampala, and as a result the hijackers released a further 101 hostages who were flown to Paris almost immediately. But when they arrived, the Israeli government were horrified to find not a single Jew amongst them. Practically every hostage now left in Entebbe was of Jewish origin.

A courtesy American AWACS reconnaissance flight had discovered two squadrons of Mig 17s and 21s sitting on the tarmac at Entebbe. Added to this, the bulk of Idi Amin's Army was only about an hour's drive away at Kampala. But irrespective of all this, the Israelis still thought it was possible to mount a successful operation to rescue the hostages.

Overall command was given to one of the country's top military men, Brigadier Dan Shonron, described by his men as the most likeable soldier in Israel. It had already been worked out that the assault troops could get to Entebbe in three C130 transport aircraft, flying in very tight formation at a height of no more than 200 feet in order to stay below the radar. These would be shielded by a Boeing 707 scheduled flight from Tel Aviv on its normal route to Kenya, which would be flying at 20,000 feet directly above them – if anything did show up on radar screens in neighbouring Arab countries, they would assume it was the scheduled flight.

Shonron's first problem would be how to deal with Uganda's overwhelming military strength on the ground. But he devised a brilliant plan, involving jeeps fixed with machine guns and an old black Mercedes, that would ensure speed and efficiency and deceive the Ugandan Army.

He divided his force into three groups. The first and largest was detailed to attack the old terminal building and provide protection for the hostages. Additionally they were to knock out the radar and communications system and deal with any Ugandan soldiers guarding the hostages. A second, smaller squad would take out the parked Migs to prevent them taking off and attacking the C130s on their return journey. The task of the third group was to set up an ambush at the entrance of the airfield to dispose of any soldiers from the nearby army camp who were attracted by the shooting and came to investigate.

One of the biggest problems that faced the whole mission was the distance involved in flying from Israel to Entebbe –

some 2,500 miles. It was almost impossible to refuel en route due to the amount of air activity that this would require. Secondly, should the C130s be spotted on Egyptian or Libyan radar despite the shield of the scheduled 707, fighters would be scrambled immediately. To offer some protection, it was decided that Israeli Mirage and Phantom fighters would escort the C130s to the limit of their range. An Israeli Air Force 707 would fly just above the scheduled 707, shielded in its radar image.

The flight path for all the aircraft would take them down the Red Sea, where they would turn right and cut across Ethiopia towards Uganda. This would send them right through the middle of potentially hostile territory. On the right they had Egypt, and on the left Saudi Arabia – both countries had sophisticated radar and missile systems in operation. Once over Uganda, the Air Force 707 would climb to 60,000 feet and circle in the 'blind zone', using highly sophisticated radar jamming equipment to block out any possibility of the operation being seen. It would also serve as an excellent communications relay, enabling the assault force on the ground to receive messages direct from Israel.

The problem of refuelling was solved – in theory anyway – by carrying refuelling equipment on board in the hope of achieving this task at Entebbe. Should this not prove possible due to lack of time, the plan was to fly on to Nairobi and hope that the Kenyans would let them in since they were on a mission of mercy. The Kenyan government had several border disputes with Idi Amin and could well be agreeable to receiving the Israelis. However, due to the tight security there was no way that they could notify the Kenyan government of the proposed attack. There was no doubt about it – fuel posed one of the biggest headaches. Weather conditions on the flight down would determine how much the C130s had left for the return journey. If Kenya refused them they could, given sufficient fuel, fly on to the Seychelles islands, a much safer bet. But would they have enough fuel to do that?

Israel called in its military élite. Every man was hand-picked from the Israeli Defence Force (IDF) – men from armoured divisions, paratroop regiments, the Golani infantry and the Special Tactics Unit operating in the Golan Heights. All of them moved into the military airbase at Sharm-El-Sheikh, where they received a full briefing and rehearsals started almost straightaway.

The man chosen by Brigadier Shonron to lead the main assault was Lieutenant Colonel Jonathan Netanyahu, a thirty-year-old American-born Jew who, like so many before him, had emigrated to Israel. 'Yoni' had been educated in both countries, had distinguished himself during the Six-Day War against Egypt, and was known throughout Israel. He was selected for his qualities of leadership, plus his rare ability to get the job done by firing his soldiers with enthusiasm.

On Friday, 2 July he rehearsed all day with his men at the airbase, where they used positions marked out in the sand to represent the buildings at Entebbe. Time after time they practised unloading the armoured jeeps from the C130s, racing across the 500 yards of tarmac and assaulting the buildings. All the men were lightly armed with Uzi machine guns and a few carried sniper rifles.

Shonron's other commanders had also been hard at work. One force had been practising setting demolition charges to deal with the Mig fighters. Another small group of about a dozen men were continually laughing – the reason became clear when they started to black their hands and faces to look like Africans. One of the Israeli soldiers, chosen especially because of his rotund girth, continued to put ever more padding around his waist to imitate the silhouette of Idi Amin. An old black Mercedes car was found and given a thorough once-over by Israeli mechanics. The finished item was made to look like a car that was currently used by Idi Amin.

At long last the Israelis were ready: the assault team and all their equipment boarded the three C130s. Soon after take-off the aircraft reached their maximum speed of just a little over 350 miles an hour. Flying at night, a few feet above the waves and relying on instruments alone, requires God on your side. The pilots were the best in Israel. They continually checked the fuel consumed by the huge Allison turbo-props, which would be running at full force for the entire journey. As they flew further south, to add to the already difficult flying conditions the weather grew worse and the C130s found it difficult to stay just above the waves of the Red Sea, or to hold their tight formation. Most of the 150 men on board were violently sick throughout the journey. Fortunately among these men were teams of paramedics and doctors, taken primarily to deal with casualties, of which the Israelis were expecting a large number. One of the C130s had been fitted with an operating theatre.

Back in Uganda, conditions had deteriorated: the toilets were blocked, the food almost inedible, and sickness and diarrhoea would soon break out. Idi Amin made several further visits to the hostages, assuring them that he was doing everything he could and that he hoped the situation would be resolved. If it wasn't, he said, then it wasn't his fault. The French pilot, Captain Michel Bacos, continued to play a dominant role in helping the hostages. He could have left with the other released passengers, but refused point blank. Both he and his crew remained with the Israelis, supporting them wholeheartedly.

The Israeli intelligence service, Mossad, had been awakening all its 'sleeping' agents in Kenya and Uganda. All were given tasks of either minor sabotage, such as cutting telephone wires, or relaying vital information to the command aircraft flying at 60,000 feet. As the rescue aircraft flew southwards, a special task force of agents left Kenya by boat, skimming across the smooth waters of Lake Victoria.

To add to the Israelis' problems, the West German government were very reluctant to hand over their six most hardened Baader-Meinhof prisoners. But they knew that if they did not, bitter resentment of Germany and a severe backlash would follow. So in the last resort, there was no doubt that the Germans would agree to hand over their terrorists in exchange for the hostages.

At about a thousand miles out the protecting Phantoms and Mirages were at the limit of their range and peeled off to return to Israel. The three C130s kept their flight pattern and, turning away from the Red Sea, flew across the mountain ranges of northern Ethiopia. As the scheduled Boeing 707 approached Nairobi, the Airforce 707 which had been flying in tandem separated from it and went directly to 60,000 feet, where it sat as planned in the blind zone so that radar would not detect it. But it would be in a perfect position to command the operation.

Two hours later the three C130s landed at Entebbe, totally unnoticed by the radar operators there. As they touched down, one of the pilots broke the radio silence and said, 'This is El- Al flight 166 with the prisoners from Tel Aviv' and, without waiting for the reply, 'Can I have permission to land?' The Entebbe control tower, taken completely unaware, was at a loss. The staff obviously knew that some arrangements had been made but had not been kept in the picture, so they had little option other than to let the flight in, thinking that only one plane had landed. Mossad agents had already cut the telephone calls to Kampala, so it was impossible to check the situation.

As the C130 taxied to the edge of the tarmac facing the old building, a large black Mercedes, complete with an escort of two Land Rovers, rolled off the tailgate at the back of the plane. This small convoy drove across the tarmac, quickly followed by Colonel Netanyahu and his men, all making

Mahmud (alias Zohair Youssif Akache) with Suhalla Saveh (alias Soraya Ansari).

The author at the bottom of the steps just after the successful GSG9 rescue.

The delivery in Dubai of a birthday cake for stewardess Gaby Dillmann, on board LH181.

Captain Shumann's body being collected from LH181 after it had been dumped on the tarmac shortly after arriving at Mogadishu.

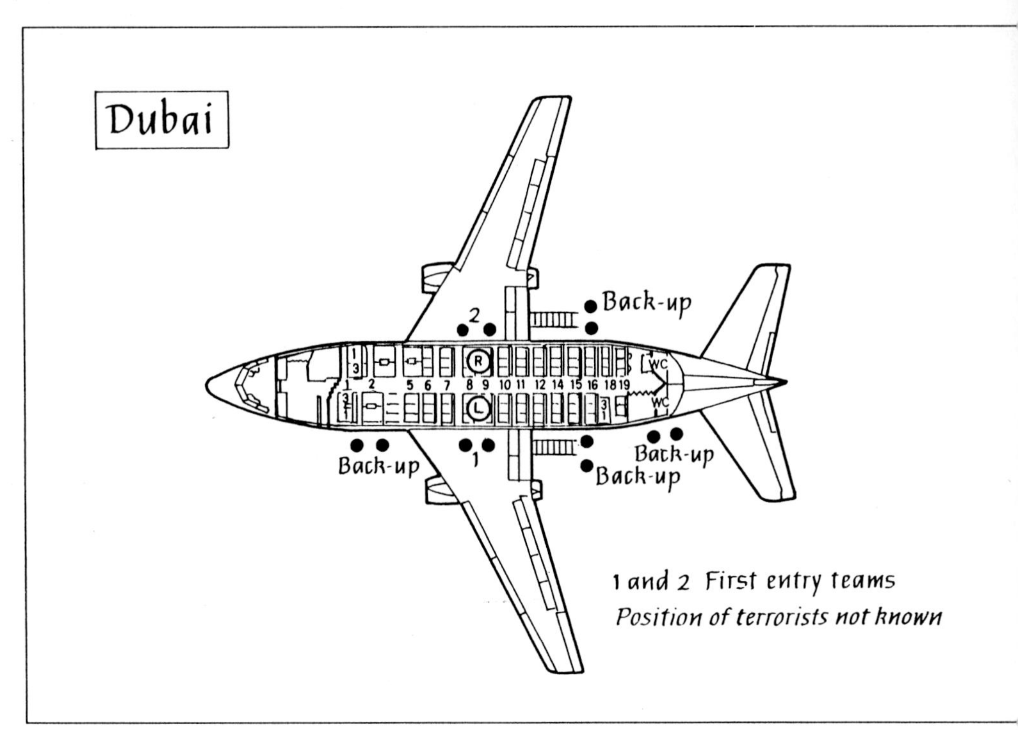

Drawing of the entry points on LH181 during abortive attempt in Dubai.

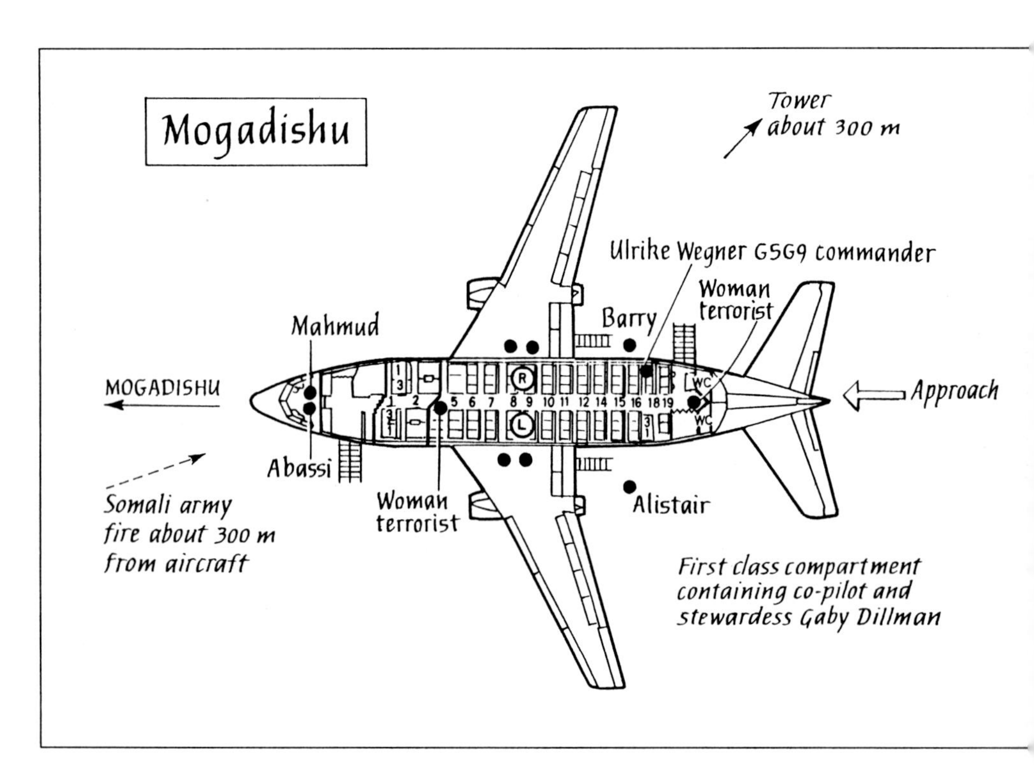

Drawing of the entry points on LH181 during actual assault in Mogadishu.

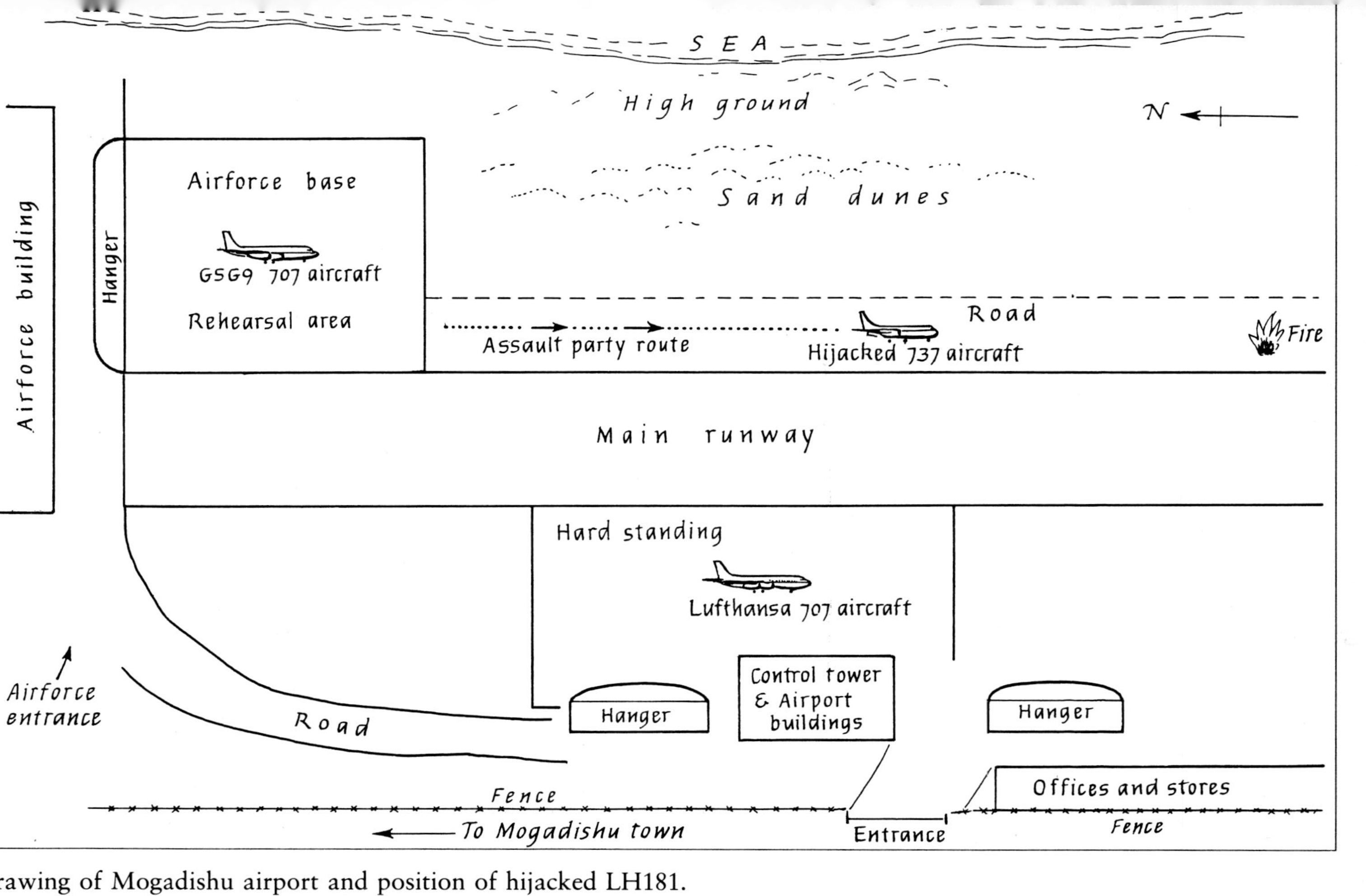

Drawing of Mogadishu airport and position of hijacked LH181.

The German beauty queens who were on board LH181.

The freed hostages arriving home in Frankfurt.

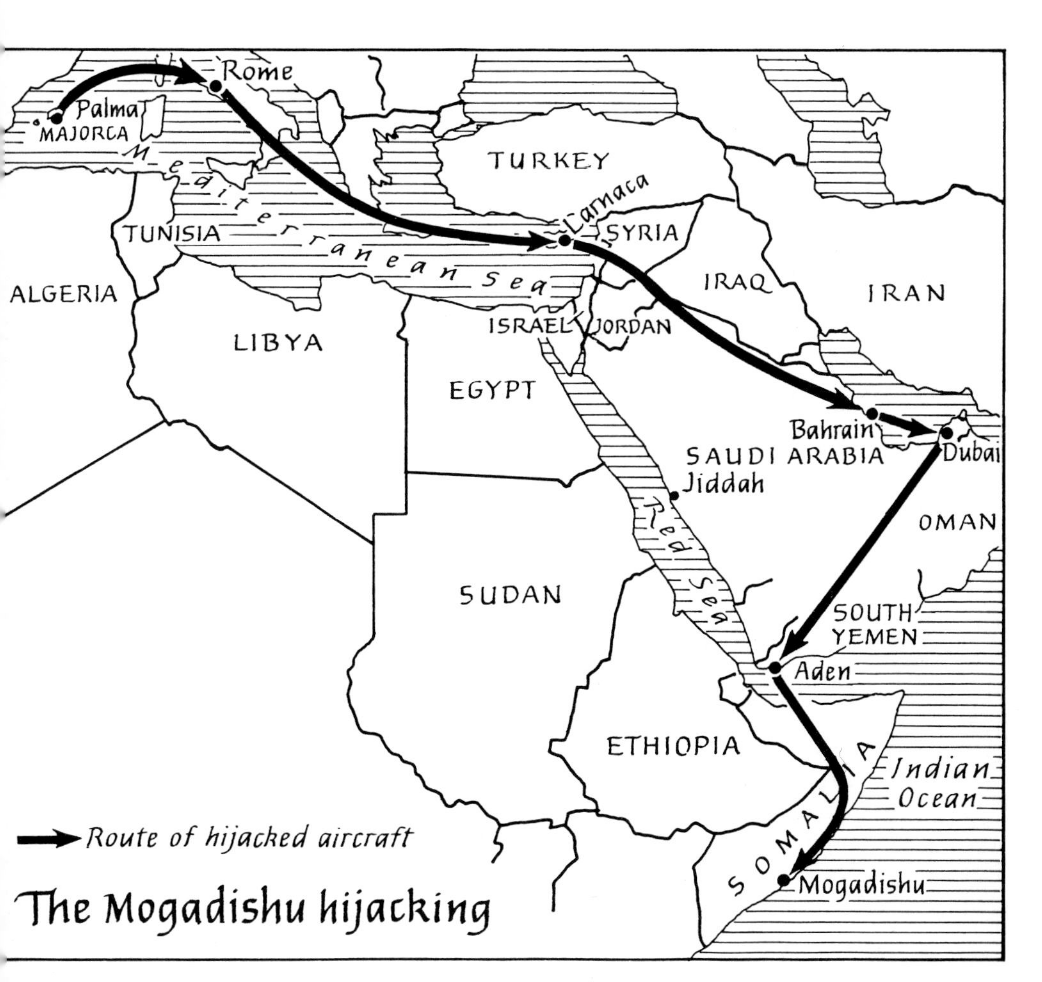

Map showing the route flown by LH181, from Palma to Mogadishu.

MINISTRY OF DEFENCE WHITEHALL LONDON SW1A 2HB

TELEPHONE 01-218 9000
DIRECT DIALLING 01-218 2111 /3

MO 21/16 20th October 1977

Dear Brigadier,

I am writing on behalf of the Prime Minister and my other Cabinet colleagues to congratulate the Special Air Service on its part in effecting the release of hostages at Mogadishu airport on Monday evening. The advice and assistance of Major Alastair Morrison and Sergeant Barry Davies made an invaluable contribution to the planning of a successful and significant operation. When the Prime Minister visited Bonn on Tuesday, Chancellor Schmidt made a point of expressing his Government's thanks for the assistance which we provided, and there is no doubt that it was very much appreciated.

I should be most grateful if you would pass on the Cabinet's sincere congratulations and thanks to Major Morrison and Sergeant Davies.

Yours sincerely

Fred Mulley

Fred Mulley

Brigadier J P B C Watts OBE MC

Letter from Fred Mulley, Ministry of Defence.

directly for the main doors of the old terminal building. Tiedemann and Boese were standing outside, together with some Ugandan officers, and were amazed to see the C130 arrive. As the convoy swept towards them the Ugandans recognised who the Mercedes was carrying and snapped smartly to attention. It was only when the convoy stopped in front of them that some of the officers realised that something was desperately wrong. By this time it was too late – the Israelis opened fire.

Boese had already guessed that there was something wrong and ran inside to fetch his machine gun. Behind him shots rang out as the men from the convoy opened fire. All around the old terminal building, small firefights broke out as soldiers from the C130 ran from the aircraft to the terminal. By the Land Rovers and the Mercedes the scene was chaotic. Men were jumping out and firing from the hip. Several Israeli soldiers armed with Galil assault rifles were sweeping the area with high-velocity automatic fire. The weight of fire put down by the Israelis was quite terrifying, but had the desired effect of driving a lot of the Ugandan soldiers back.

Gabrielle Tiedemann raised her pistol and managed to fire one shot before she was cut down. Boese had now found his machine gun, and several of the hostages watched in horror as he pointed it at them. Then he turned, without firing, and ran outside. As he emerged, Boese decided to surrender and threw his gun in front of him, thrusting his arms into the air. A burst of automatic fire killed him instantly.

By now, Colonel Netanyahu and his soldiers were well inside the building and shouting to the hostages: 'Stay down! Stay down!' Another group of Yoni's men trapped the two PFLP terrorists in an upstairs room, but had difficulty killing them. Every time they went into the room they got fired at, so eventually they threw in a grenade and finished the Arabs off. Another group took out the terminal and killed the Ugandan soldiers there. Despite all the shooting, the three Ugandan radar operators were not harmed and were merely locked in a separate room.

As the firefight continued, the Ugandan soldiers started to regroup and attack. By this stage Yoni had started organising the evacuation of the hostages from the building into the aircraft – suddenly a shot rang out and he was hit badly in the back. He died a few moments later. Immediately the news was flashed to Israel via the Airforce 707 mobile command post flying above Entebbe that their hero Colonel Yoni Netanyahu was dead.

The second C130 had landed just a few seconds after the first, and instantly one group had gone off to attack the new airport building. The second group had gone off to deal with the Migs. Now huge fireballs erupted into the sky as the fighters were destroyed on the ground. Another group had gone to the main entrance gate and met up with the Mossad agents, who had already prepared an ambush for any support coming from the Ugandan barracks a few hundred yards away.

Slowly, but surely, the whole situation came under control, and the hostages were taken across the tarmac and put aboard the C130s. The engineers aboard had removed the pumping equipment and were working furiously to fill the empty tanks of the C130s.

As the soldiers loaded the hostages on board the planes, the paramedics and doctors rushed to treat the wounded. Meticulously, all the hostages and soldiers were counted, making sure that no one was left behind. Even the Land Rovers and the Mercedes were put on board and returned to Israel. As the three aircraft took off, they left behind them a ruined airport terminal, two squadrons of Mig 21s and 17s totally destroyed, and over a hundred Ugandan soldiers dead or dying in the darkness. The whole operation had taken no more than ninety-five minutes. Once more, the C130s flew up the Red Sea towards Israel, as squadrons of Phantoms and

Mirages were scrambled to give them maximum air cover. Mission completed, the Israelis were going home.

This was the first time that any government had stood up to hijackers and used a brilliantly conceived and executed commando-style operation to release hostages. Others would follow, with varying degrees of success. Among them was the assault on the hijacked LH181, which on Thursday, 13 October 1977 was en route from Majorca to Frankfurt carrying a crew of five and eighty-six passengers, only four of whom knew anything of the violence that was about to erupt.

11

THE TAKING OF LH181

The Lufthansa jet was named *Landshut* after a pretty little village in eastern Bavaria, but was officially known as flight number LH181 from Palma-Majorca to Frankfurt, West Germany, departing at 1pm. The crew consisted of Captain Jürgen Schumann, an ex-Starfighter pilot, Jürgen Vietor, his co-pilot, and three stewardesses, Hannelore Piegler, Gaby Dillmann and Anna-Maria Staringer.

Life seemed normal and relaxed as LH181 took off from Palma – only the eleven German beauty queens on board attracted any particular attention amongst the passengers. As the aircraft reached its cruising altitude, the stewardesses settled into their duties, preparing for the in-flight meal.

Suddenly, stewardess Piegler heard some disturbing noises coming from the main cabin and went forward to investigate. As she pulled back the curtain that separated first class from economy she received a vicious blow that sent her reeling backwards. Although dazed, she noticed that a man standing by the cockpit door was brandishing a gun. The woman who had been seated next to him now stood up, clasping two grenades, and started screaming for the passengers to put up their hands. Similar cries were coming from economy class, and stewardess Piegler turned to see two more terrorists step into the aisle, with guns and grenades.

Hysteria spread through the aircraft, and the terrorists shouting for control did little to calm the terrified passengers. The two women, Soraya and Shahnaz, were in charge of the passengers while Mahmud went forward to the flight deck and took over the loudspeaker. The co-pilot Jürgen Vietor, the stewardesses and the first-class passengers were herded back into economy-class seats by the other terrorist.

Over the loudspeaker came a male voice, demanding in passable English that everyone put their hands up and comply with the orders of his officers. Very slowly calm descended on the fearful passengers, and the terrorists in the aisle stopped shouting. Now, confidently, the speaker informed them that the aircraft had been taken over by Captain Martyr Mahmud.

What should have been a journey of two hours was now to last five days. Those five days were filled with fatigue, death and disorientation as the hijacked aircraft flew erratically around the Mediterranean, coming to rest first in the heat of the Middle Eastern desert and finally on the shores of East Africa.

Once the initial shock was over, Captain Schumann relaxed as far as possible and implemented Lufthansa's policy on hijacks – basically the same as for all major airlines: avoid violence at all costs, stall for time, co-operate fully with the terrorists and reassure the passengers. Schumann seemed to have dealt well with the emotional side, and there is little doubt that whenever he could he passed vital information to the authorities. The following day's news reports stated that the aircraft had been hijacked by two men and two women. It was never properly established how he conveyed these details. Some reports say that he put four cigarettes in a box when some of the rubbish was taken from the aircraft in Dubai. Comments made later by Sheikh Mohammed of the Dubai authorities suggest that Schumann may have used some kind of code in their conversation. Whatever he did, it was a brilliant job.

The new route taken by the hijacked aircraft led it from Palma towards Rome, where it touched down at 3.45pm. Here Mahmud issued his demands to the control tower, which were to be transmitted to Bonn. The demands were almost identical to those made for Hans-Martin Schleyer: the release of the eleven Baader-Meinhof prisoners, with the addition of two Palestinians held in Turkish jails and the sum of $15 million.

At 5.50 local time, after being refuelled, without permission, the jet took off. Captain Schumann informed the Rome control tower that he was headed for Cyprus. Some three hours later the hijacked aircraft touched down at Larnaca.

Since the kidnapping of Hans-Martin Schleyer the West German Minister of State Wischnewski had been tirelessly visiting all those countries that might possibly accept the terrorists, in an attempt to persuade them either to co-operate with his government or at least not to assist the terrorists. So there were now potential friends in all sorts of unlikely places. One such source of assistance was Cyprus. Here a member of the Palestine Liberation Organisation (PLO), Zakaria Abdel Rahim, tried in vain to talk to Mahmud (his failure to do so highlighted the massive rift between the PLO and more extreme groups). Eventually, Mahmud did talk to Rahim, but only to give him a mouthful of rhetoric outlining what he thought of the PLO. Requests for the release of the women and children fell on deafears. Shortly afterwards Mahmud broke contact with Abdel Rahim and demanded eleven tons of fuel together with the weather report for Beirut. The Cypriot authorities skilfully kept up a dialogue with Mahmud, desperately trying to delay the aircraft, thus giving the West German government time to despatch their anti-terrorist force, the GSG9 to Cyprus.

The GSG9 had been on stand-by since the start of the hijack, but had never been used before and as a result the government found itself enmeshed in departmental bureaucracy. It took vital hours before official permission for them to go in was granted. The tragic result was that their Boeing 707 did not arrive in Larnaca until two hours after the hijacked aircraft had left.

LH181 took off at 10.50pm and flew to Beirut, but they were refused entry and the same thing happened in Damascus. Some eighty miles out of Bahrain, with very little fuel, Captain Schumann requested permission to land – once again this was denied. Luckily, by accident or design the authorities in Bahrain had forgotten to switch off the IMF auto-landing equipment, and Captain Schumann managed to land his aircraft safely with just three minutes' fuel spare.

As the hijacked aircraft taxied to a halt the terrorist leader Mahmud started talking to the control tower, refusing to negotiate and demanding fuel. At this stage armed troops appeared and surrounded the aircraft. When he saw them Mahmud feared an attack on the aircraft and threatened to shoot the co-pilot, Jürgen Vietor.

As Mahmud pushed his pistol against Vietor's temple he screamed into the microphone, demanding that the soldiers be pulled back within five minutes or he would carry out his threat. As the minutes ticked away Vietor realised that Mahmud was serious about shooting him and begged for permission to speak to the control tower himself, pleading with Mahmud that he had a wife and children. With two minutes to go the co-pilot appealed for his life.

'Hello, control tower, this is the co-pilot, Jürgen Vietor. There is a man next to me with a gun at my head. If you do not withdraw your soldiers immediately, he will shoot me.'

Captain Schumann likewise voiced his opinion. 'There is no point in all this, it would be senseless to kill him.'

As he pleaded, the co-pilot exclaimed with relief: 'They're pulling back!' Suddenly the situation relaxed and, once refuelled, the aircraft took off heading in the direction of Dubai.

At 6am the aircraft touched down at Dubai and immediately taxied to the far end of the old airport. The hijack was now seventeen hours old. Shortly afterwards, Mahmud issued his first deadline for the release of the Baader-Meinhof. It was set at midday GMT on Sunday, 16 October.

As the blinds on the aircraft had been drawn across the porthole windows it was impossible for the passengers to know exactly where they were, and the numerous landings and take-offs had totally disorientated them. However, when they did receive a meal, it must have been of some comfort to find that the food boxes bore the words 'Dubai Airport'. At least they would feel fairly safe in the hands of a pro-Western sheikhdom.

But on the plane itself they were still at the mercy of the hijackers, who now collected all the passports and examined the names on them. Believing they had three Jewish women on board, they started to interrogate them behind the closed curtains of the first-class compartment. Fellow passengers reported hearing crashes and bumps, and said that the women returned looking shaken and very disturbed.

Around this time, totally unnoticed by the hijackers, a Lufthansa Boeing 707 had landed in Dubai. This was a negotiating aircraft used by German Minister of State Wischnewski. Amongst his companions were a psychologist named Wolfgang Salewsky, Chancellor Schmidt's adviser on the Schleyer kidnapping. Despite Wischnewski's plea to be allowed to bring in the GSG9, the Sheikh of Dubai declined. All command and decisions over the hijack had been delegated to his son, Sheikh Mohammed, who was the state's Defence Minister, and if any military action was indeed needed, he declared, Dubai troops would undertake it.

After a restless night, Sunday morning found both terrorists and hostages in a more cheerful mood. A catering truck had arrived a little after 8am and the stewardesses dispensed breakfast. As they were doing so the Norwegian stewardess, Anna-Maria Staringer, said that it was her birthday. When Mahmud discovered this he said, 'We shall celebrate and have a cake and champagne.'

Enthused with his own idea, Mahmud made his demands of Sheikh Mohammed in the control tower. Around lunchtime Staringer received her birthday cake and a case of champagne, and both terrorists and hostages held a somewhat bizarre celebration.

At one stage Mahmud – still looking calm and rational – picked up the microphone and asked in English for silence. He then proceeded to give an hour-long lecture on the history of Palestine. The Palestinians, Mahmud said, had lived in their homeland on the banks of the Jordan for two thousand years. Then the British, in conjunction with world imperialism, had decided that the Palestinians had to give up their lands to the Zionists. As Mahmud went on his voice grew more and more excited, and then suddenly a shot rang out. For a few seconds everyone held their breath, thinking that Mahmud had shot someone. But all that had happened was that the pistol in his hand had gone off accidentally. Much later, several of the passengers and crew stated that initially Mahmud's rhetoric was sheer garbage, but as he talked they came to realise how little they knew about the reality of the Palestinian situation. Several felt that, should they get out of the hijack situation safely, they would make time to explore and understand the problem.

Shortly afterwards Mahmud went back to his hostile mode. Normally in a hijack or kidnap situation, after a day or so it is not uncommon for terrorists and hostages to build up some kind of rapport. But on LH181 the terrorists showed little or no sign of doing so. As the characters of the individual hijackers started to emerge, the hostages began to learn who to trust and who to fear. Afterwards, many of them described the two women as firm but polite, and the shorter of the two men as fairly easy-going. During their presence the passengers could relax a little and on occasion were allowed to stretch their legs or use the toilet. But when Mahmud appeared, the whole atmosphere changed.

One passenger, Hautwig Faby, a twenty-seven-year-old schoolteacher, recalls that Mahmud was always coming into the economy-class compartment in an emotional state bordering on hysteria. 'Every time he came into our section we were afraid,' she said. 'He even told the children, "If you don't stop chattering, I will blow your heads off."'

The immediate shock of being hijacked wore off after a few hours. But as time dragged on the small things started to build up and increased the strain of captivity. Access to the toilets was restricted, the passengers had to remain in their seats, and routine activities such as eating and washing did not take place in their normal way. All this created stress and tension and heightened the sense of danger.

At this stage the temperature in the plane was quite bearable as the air conditioning was still running, but the system needed power. Jürgen Schumann had worked out exactly how much fuel he had left, and estimated that he had enough to run the auxiliary power unit (APU) for another twelve hours. This meant that some time during that evening the electricity would fail and with it the air conditioning unit. Realising the discomfort and panic that this might cause, he warned Mahmud of the situation. Mahmud's response was that they should take on more fuel. This request had already been made, replied Schumann, but Sheikh Mohammed had refused to comply unless the women and children were released.

Some hours later the last drop of fuel ran out as expected and the aircraft's lighting and air conditioning ceased to function. The terrorists now found it very difficult to control all the hostages and were afraid of an attack under cover of darkness. For the passengers, too, sitting in the dark and silence must have increased the tension tenfold. To ease the situation, Schumann immediately switched to the stand-by batteries, intended to give the plane an extra half hour of air if the generator broke down in flight. But after this the temperature inside the cabin rose minute by minute, and soon it was an unbearable 120 degrees Fahrenheit. The passengers started to faint, and in an effort to try and reduce the air temperature a little Mahmud ordered that the doors on the port side, both front and rear, should be opened. Again Mahmud demanded fuel of the control tower. Eventually a tanker drove up, and two men attached a pipe under the wing in preparation for filling the tank under pressure. But unfortunately the 800 litres of fuel that were put into the aircraft went into the wrong wing – the APU generator feeds from the starboard side only. With the batteries now almost dead, there was no power to transfer-pump the fuel from one wing to the other.

The conditions inside the cabin were now becoming critical, and the young and old especially were feeling particularly weak. Most of the passengers removed their shirts or blouses. Although they understood why the passengers had done so, Mahmud and the other terrorists were not comfortable with this state of undress – despite the death and violence caused by the PFLP, their personal moral standards were very high.

A little while later, two men drove from the terminal building in a small tow-truck, which was pulling a ground power unit. But as they approached within earshot of the hijacked aircraft, Mahmud heard them speaking German. It was possible that they were the pilots of the 707 that had brought Minister Wischnewski and his team to Dubai. Quickly, Schumann pointed out to Mahmud that, unless they had some kind of power, within a few hours there would be no need for anyone to blow up the plane – the passengers would die of heat exhaustion. But Mahmud was still highly suspicious of the two men who had come to fix the unit, and fired off several shots. The men ran off, leaving the unit behind.

Shortly afterwards the co-pilot, Jürgen Vietor, was lowered to the ground and managed to attach the unit. While Vietor was outside, Mahmud became very angry with Schumann and accused him of passing information to the tower. He made Schumann march up and down the aisle, and then interrogated him in front of the passengers.

'If you do not tell me the truth, I will shoot out your eyes, first the left one, then the right. You have told them there are four of us?'

'Yes,' replied Schumann.

'You have told them what weapons we have?'

'Yes, two pistols, four grenades and explosives.'

'This man is the enemy. He has betrayed you. He now admits his guilt,' Mahmud addressed everybody. 'No one will speak to this man – no one.'

Minutes before the sun started to rise in the clear Arabian sky the air conditioning cut back in.

12

SAS ENTER THE ARENA

On the morning of Monday, 10 October 1977, four days before the hijacking of LH181, I had taken a team of ten SAS anti-terrorist members to Heathrow for some on-the-spot training in airport layouts and routines. On the first day we were briefed at the main airport police station, where we attended lectures and watched various films on aircraft disasters. Although these were of little use with regard to anti-terrorist techniques, they did provide us with an excellent insight into the way the emergency services operate.

The following day we divided ourselves into groups and toured the airport, assessing the security methods employed by the airport authority and the different airlines. It is often difficult to employ really strict security at all major points, given the number of people moving through the airport at any one time, but despite this most of what we observed was excellent. By far the best was the security system employed by El-Al, the official Israeli airline. It was done in a logical way from start to finish, with check-in procedures locked down tight, and was most impressive.

All day Wednesday and Thursday morning were spent crawling over miscellaneous aircraft, familiarising ourselves with their internal layouts and the variations employed by different major airlines. Most of this work was accomplished during the periods allowed for cleaning between scheduled flights. Equipped in cleaners' overalls, we had the run of the airport.

Again, El-Al surprised me. Due to the constant threat of hijackings, some airlines were employing 'sky marshals' – men who were normally armed during the flight. However, due to the British firearms restrictions all weapons had to be placed in a locked metal box fastened to the aircraft floor. This procedure came into effect the moment the aircraft landed. But when we examined an El-Al box we discovered that, although the box was firmly secured with a padlock, the hinges at the back of the lid could be pushed out in the event of an emergency to give access to the weapons. I like that kind of foresight.

On Thursday evening we all gathered at the Three Magpies pub, which backs on to the police station at Heathrow, for a farewell drink with some of the police and dog handlers whom we had got to know. As we sat there, the first news started to filter through that there had been a hijack of a Lufthansa aircraft, but we paid it scant attention.

That night one of my guys called 'Nobby', owing to the fact that he had lost a testicle playing football in his early military career, made off with one of the young policewomen. Next morning, after checking out of our accommodation in Hounslow, we returned to the police station to say our good-byes and wait for Nobby, who did not return until about 10.30. During this time, I read the front page of *The Times* and the small section describing how a Lufthansa Boeing 737 had been hijacked by two men and two women. The main feature seemed to be that there were eleven beauty queens on board, who had won free flights to Palma Nova.

Normally, Nobby's lateness would have automatically resulted in a fine donated by the perpetrator to Squadron Funds, but I decided to let him off this time. The journey back to Hereford was slow and tedious, due to the thickening fog. Never mind, Nobby kept us amused with the exaggerated tales of his bedroom exploits. As usual he included his favourite story, which consisted of his trick of pretending to search the lady's bed. When asked by the young woman what was he looking for, he would proudly stand up and show off his one testicle, complaining that he had two when he originally climbed into her bed.

Little did I know that as we drove back to Hereford, dramatic telephone calls were being made from Germany to England, and that I would be immediately recalled to London. But by the end of Friday, after I had been rushed by helicopter to London to attend a briefing on the situation with military top brass, Lufthansa flight LH181 had become number one priority in my life.

Outside the door of No. 10 a chauffeured government car waited to drive the SAS second-in-command, Major Alastair Morrison, and me to Brize Norton airbase in Oxfordshire, from where we would be flown to Germany. The thick fog made it a slow and tedious drive, and we finally arrived at Brize Norton at about four in the morning. At the guard room we met up with the lads from Hereford whom I had earlier phoned and asked to deliver the stun grenades which the Germans needed. I quickly checked them and satisfied myself that they were of the correct type. Such is the professionalism of the SAS that the lads never asked me what was going on, and I did not tell them.

We were then directed to the cook-house, where we met the stand-by crew of the C130 which had been placed at our disposal, ready for immediate take-off once those in authority had given permission. Major Morrison told the duty station officer in no uncertain terms that this operation came directly under the orders of the Prime Minister and that we were to depart directly. Because of the fog it was, however, explained that certain procedures had to be in place before the C130 would be allowed to leave.

Taking advantage of this short break we ate a quick breakfast with the air crew, who seemed very excited about their early morning mission. I asked the RAF police to secure the box containing the stun grenades on the C130 along with my bag – still containing the dirty washing from my Heathrow trip – and to keep them under close guard. Major Morrison and I waited another half hour as the low-level radar system was scrambled into operation, which would allow our aircraft to cross into Germany no matter what the weather conditions. While we waited, I got to catching up on all the gossip from the second-in-command, Major Alastair Morrison OBE MC. I had known Alastair from when he had joined the SAS from the Scots Guards. He originally joined the Squadron and commanded the Mobility Troop, they are the ones who drive the 'Pinkys'. (That's a cut-down Landrover painted pink and equipped with enough fire power to start a small war.) You may be interested to know that Free Fall Troop's commander at the time was a young Captain called Mike Rose.

As the C130 thundered down the runway and lifted off, I checked the box of grenades and again was happy to see that the lads had enclosed four of the new trembler devices. As I did this one of the RAF pilots came to look over my shoulder. When he saw the contents of the box his eyes widened and he asked, 'Are those the fuses for nuclear bombs?'

'Why else would the Prime Minister order an aircraft to fly in these conditions at this level and at this hour?' I said with a straight face, packing the box back into my bag of dirty washing.

He rapidly made his way back to the flight deck to convey the news – some people will believe anything.

There was little else to do now so I stretched myself out on the canvas parachute seats and wrapped my coat around me, and seconds later I was asleep – I have a wonderful in-built ability to fall asleep at will. Alastair Morrison woke me about ten minutes before the C130 landed at Bonn. It was 6.30am on Saturday, 15 October. The two GSG9 members we had met and talked to in London were there to greet us. Hastily Morrison and I were bundled into a GSG9 Mercedes and driven directly to their barracks headquarters in St Augstin. Here we met their second-in-command, Major Bletter, who gave us an accurate briefing on the situation in Dubai. He also informed us that the GSG9 commander, Ulrich Wegener, and other personnel had flown out to Dubai with Minister of State Wischnewski aboard a Lufthansa 707 jet.

Major Bletter was intrigued about the stun grenades and wanted to see them in operation, so we decided to stage a demonstration. I needed a space similar in size and shape to the interior of an aircraft, and found a long corridor in the cellars of the GSG9 building. It took some persuasion to get a dozen nervous GSG9 men to take up positions in various recessed doorways. With suspicious eyes, they watched me as I unclipped the metal box and withdrew one of the menacing black rubber cylinders. Continually assuring the GSG9 men that it would not harm them (sometimes I have a wicked sense of humour!) I switched off the lights, pulled out the pin and tossed the grenade into the darkness amongst them. The delay is about .8 of a second, and no matter how many times you practise with stun grenades in training, when you are on the receiving end of a live one the effect is devastating. The language was pretty blue as several severely shocked GSG9 men emerged staggering from the cellar corridor!

After the demonstration, the second-in-command of GSG9 decided to send Morrison and me on to Dubai by the fastest means. Unfortunately, the first plane we could get was the midday Kuwaiti Airways flight out of Frankfurt. We would have to transfer to another plane in Kuwait.

All went smoothly until we arrived at Kuwait Airport.

The entire Middle East was alarmed by the Dubai hijack, and the airport was on full military alert with soldiers stationed everywhere. Then we discovered that even passengers in transit were having their luggage checked before being allowed on board the Dubai plane. And here was I with one small bag full of dirty, and by now somewhat smelly, washing which concealed a metal box containing seven top-secret stun grenades!

Major Morrison (whom I shall sometimes refer to as the 'boss' or Alastair – in the SAS, it's a sign of respect for officers when first names are used by other ranks) went off to find the Lufthansa general manager. As we left Germany we had been told that GSG9 would radio ahead and tell the manager to render any assistance necessary. After a brief discussion, the boss persuaded him to clear us through the security check, which he set off to do.

Our flight was called and we joined the line that led to the X-ray machine. When my turn came I plonked the bag squarely in front of the Arab operator. I thought at first that he must have looked at so many bags that day that he might let it slip by – wrong, in the green silhouette of my bag the shape of the metal box with its cargo of cylinder-like objects stood out like balls on a billiard table.

The Arab looked at me, I looked at the Arab, and he went berserk – screaming and jumping down from his seat, he pointed at the boss and me as if he had just caught us in bed screwing his wife. For a moment no one moved, then rifle-bearing Kuwaiti soldiers surrounded us and a very nasty-looking bayonet was shoved in my face. After that we were manhandled quite ruthlessly into the chief security officer's room. Gingerly, someone removed my bag from the X-ray machine and delivered it to the room.

In Britain, if something like this happens it's done in an orderly fashion, with a policeman stationed at the door to make sure no one gets in. Not in Kuwait. The room seemed to fill very quickly, and gaping eyes watched as my bag was opened for examination. Kneeling in front of the security officer's desk was an old Arab – obviously expendable. He now removed the box, which had '9mm ammunition' marked all over it, from among my soiled underwear. Without hesitation he flipped open the lid and withdrew one of the black rubber cylinders; there were more gasps of wonder from the assembled crowd. Just as the old guy looked as if he was about to pull the pin I leaped out of my seat, threw both my arms up in horror and yelled: 'Stop!'

It worked. First they all looked at me, then they looked at the old man holding the grenade, then, amid screams and shouts, the room emptied. That is not strictly true – the boss and I stood our ground, the old Arab froze rigid and the security officer was trapped behind his desk. The tableau was broken by the sudden reappearance of the Lufthansa manager. This German was taking no prisoners. He entered the room and issued the security officer with an ultimatum: if Alastair and I were not allowed back on to the aircraft with the grenades right now, no German aircraft would ever land in Kuwait again.

'Who are they?' the frightened security officer enquired, 'and what are those?' pointing at the stun grenades.

The boss cut in, 'We are travelling to Dubai at the request of the German government, and these are communication devices for sticking to the outside of aircraft in order to overhear any conversation inside.'

The Kuwaiti security guy was out of his league on this one, and he knew it. My Arabic is not very good, but he made a few remarks regarding our mothers and heritage, then promptly dismissed us. I rapidly took the grenade from the hands of the still rigid old man and closed my bag. The boss and I went straight to the waiting aircraft, with Kuwaiti soldiers escorting us across the tarmac at bayonet point. Two passengers were forcibly removed while the boss and I were physically pushed into their seats; one soldier insisted that I nurse my bag containing the grenades on my lap. I was starting to get pissed off by now, and explained in my finest Arabic what I would do to him if he didn't take his bad breath and acne out of my face. To our relief, a few moments later the aircraft took off for Dubai.

'That was close, I had visions of you and I spending the rest of our lives in a Kuwaiti prison,' said Alastair.

'Don't remind me, I once saw an English guy in an Arab jail. If he was lucky they would beam sunlight down to him with a mirror every Friday,' I replied jokingly. 'Can you imagine what would have happened if they had set off a stun grenade?' At this we both laughed and settled down. I had calmed down a little by now, and took stock of our situation. Everything was back to normal, well almost.

Now ordinarily, with nothing to do, I would just fall asleep, but I was puzzled. I have flown on a lot of aircraft in my life and some have been pretty full, but this aircraft had a surplus – at least ten people were actually sitting in the aisle. The situation was explained a few moments later when the Captain announced that this flight was headed for Dubai and not Karachi. This news seemed to come as a bit of a shock for the group of Indians sitting at the rear of the aircraft. There is always someone worse off than yourself. I went to sleep.

13

MISSED OPPORTUNITY

We arrived in Dubai at around 2am on Sunday the 16th, a few hours before the terrorists' first deadline, which was set at noon that day. Problems started for Alastair and me the moment we arrived at passport control, where we were detained due to lack of proper documentation. The boss explained that we had come to help in the hijack situation, but to no avail – we were held kicking our heels impatiently in a transit lounge as our passports disappeared for examination.

As the official walked away I noticed a European go up and speak to him. I believe this man was a Reuters reporter, who had just arrived on the same flight and must have witnessed the commotion in Kuwait. From the passports he obtained our names, plus the fact that they had 'Government Service' stamped on them. Putting two and two together, he assumed that we were somehow connected with the hijack, which is why both our names appeared in the press the following day.

Security, as expected, was very tight at Dubai Airport, although at this stage no one had bothered to check my bag of dirty washing which contained the stun grenades. Despite the alert, normal scheduled air traffic was allowed to arrive and depart as usual. This was possible because the hijacked aircraft was isolated a mile away on an old piece of runway, far removed from the modern glass and steel complex that made up the new airport of this oil-rich sheikhdom. Even so, LH181 was in full view of the control tower from where the negotiations were now taking place. The Dubai authorities were taking no chances, for despite its distance from the new buildings the plane stood within two hundred metres of the perimeter fence. Between the fence and LH181 soldiers of the Dubai Defence Force (DDF) now lay hidden in the low sand-dunes that surrounded the aircraft on three sides and gave them excellent cover. As we waited I thought of the hostages on board – even though they still had electricity to keep the cabin temperature down in the blistering heat of the day, conditions would already be pretty unpleasant as the toilets became blocked, and food and drink would only be available at the hijackers' whim.

The boss made numerous attempts to contact the British Consulate, but could not get past the switchboard, which was continually answered by some man with a very sleepy voice. Then luck smiled on us: we saw a European officer whom we recognised. It was David Bullied, an ex-SAS man working under contract for the Dubai Palace Guard. From that point, events took a completely different turn. Without David's help, at that moment and subsequently throughout the rescue operation, we might never have achieved the success that we did. He proved absolutely indispensable to us.

David had served as a troop commander with the SAS a few years before, and since leaving had been seconded to the Dubai Defence Force. As the SAS trained the soldiers of the Palace Guard, David found himself working with them. One great advantage was that he had a lot of muscle with the Defence Minister, Sheikh Mohammed bin Rachid, the man now in charge of dealing with the hijack in Dubai. David suggested introducing us to the Sheikh, so, brushing aside protests from immigration, and under his protection, we regained our passports and made our way to the control tower.

As we walked, David admitted that the Dubai Defence Force had put together a spontaneous team that could storm the aircraft if the terrorists started to shoot hostages. He stressed that the men were working in the dark and had no previous training in anti-terrorist drills. David was extremely helpful in many other ways – for instance, he had already primed some of the best soldiers from the Palace Guard to assist us. Should things escalate and the terrorists start to shoot the hostages systematically, we would need all the immediate help we could get. Also, his position within the Dubai military structure allowed him – and subsequently the boss and me – great freedom around the airport.

When we entered the control tower, the green glow of the radar panels reflected in the darkness of the shadowy tower, creating an atmosphere of reassuring efficiency. But although the atmosphere was calm, I was surprised at the unusually large number of people crammed into the tower. Apart from the normal staff there were a number of people who had just come for a look, including a guy selling bottles of Coke. Additionally there were several prominent people in attendance, who included Sheikh Mohammed. David Bullied introduced us, explaining that we were SAS specialists and that the British Prime Minister had sent us to lend assistance.

Also in the packed control tower we met Minister Wischnewski, the German government's principal representative in the hijack affair. Herr Wischnewski was a short, stocky man with a typically efficient German attitude, and was plainly a man of action. I learned later how he had been working almost non-stop since the kidnapping of Hans-Martin Schleyer, visiting most of the countries elected by the terrorists for sanctuary. His ploy had been the same with all of them. 'If you support the terrorists, you will feel the wrath of Germany's industrial might.' The more I watched Herr Wischnewski the more I came to respect him; his energy seemed unlimited, and as a diplomat he was outstanding. Especially towards the end of our war of nerves, his decision-making was always clear, concise and very rapid.

However, from what we could gather it would seem that the Germans were not having much luck trying to persuade Sheikh Mohammed to let them bring in the GSG9 anti-terrorist team. But Sheikh Mohammed was doing an excellent job of negotiation with the terrorist leader Mahmud, holding a firm but steady dialogue. 'We know what makes him nervous and how to calm him down,' he told us. 'I don't think he will blow up the plane, but he may start harming people.' Sheikh Mohammed had dealt with hijacks before and he fully understood the risks – especially with people like Mahmud, whom he later described as 'mentally unstable and very dangerous'. During one conversation Sheikh Mohammed said to Mahmud, 'In the name of merciful Allah, let the *children* go.' Mahmud refused point-blank, giving not one inch of ground.

We then set off in search of the GSG9 commander, who had arrived earlier. Eventually we found him and some of his men in the VIP lounge, sitting around a table talking. They seemed delighted to see us, having been notified of our imminent arrival by their headquarters, in Germany. One of the first things they mentioned were the stun grenades – it was nice to know that my small demonstration had had some lasting effect!

Ulrich Wegener, David Bullied, the boss and I set about discussing what, if anything, we could do in Dubai. The boss suggested that, in case the terrorists started to shoot hostages, we should set about training an ad hoc team. If we all participated together we would have some chance of success, and if we demonstrated the possibilities to Sheikh Mohammed he might favour an assault on the plane. If we could persuade him that the mechanics of anti-hijacking techniques worked well he might also allow the GSG9 main team into Dubai. It was agreed.

So we devised a basic plan to attack the aircraft here in Dubai. It would entail using the three GSG9, three European officers seconded to the DDF, two members of the Palace Guard, the boss and me. The Germans were not too happy about using the two Arabs from the Palace Guard, but Sheikh Mohammed was most insistent that if any attack on the aircraft was to take place in Dubai his own forces must be involved.

After a while we agreed that there was little we could do until the morning, and we all needed some sleep. It was decided that the Germans should go and stay at a nearby hotel, which David duly arranged, while the boss and I went home with David. We arranged to meet again in a few hours' time to draw up a more detailed plan which could be used to assault the aircraft with the force now available.

Luckily, David's comfortable home was only a few minutes from the airport. His wife plied us with scrambled eggs and coffee while we discussed our plan of action. At this stage I did most of the talking, as we were getting to the hands-on stage. David made furiously scribbled notes, as well as lists of required kit and equipment which seemed to grow ever longer. Our most expensive request was for the use of a 737 aircraft – this was essential for training and practice if we were to stand any chance of success. Around 5am we all went to bed – except for the tireless David Bullied, who left to make further arrangements. A couple of hours later, as the boss and I, much refreshed, were having breakfast, he returned with the news that he had managed to fulfil most of our equipment demands and it was now being assembled at the airport. Shortly afterwards all three of us left to rendezvous with Ulrich Wegener again.

We assembled by a very large hangar out of sight of the hijacked aircraft and the media. Surprise, surprise, parked on the hard standing was a Gulf Air 737 jet which had been commandeered by Sheikh Mohammed for our sole use! Much of the equipment we had specified just a few hours earlier now lay piled high on the hangar floor. The first priority was to check it all; not that I needed to worry – David introduced me to a quartermaster, again a seconded British soldier. He was standing by the hangar doors and beside him were three Land Rovers. He was clutching a wad of money thick enough to choke a camel. As I requested more equipment he would simply flip off a quantity of notes from this huge wad and despatch a man in a Land Rover to buy the required items.

Now it was time for me to earn my pay. I had no knowledge of how good the GSG9 were, and as we were assembling an improvised team I felt I was the one best qualified to organise the training. So, gathering everyone around me in a semicircle, I set about explaining an immediate action drill designed to meet the needs of the worst possible scenario. This would be if and when the terrorists started killing hostages en masse, when we would have no choice other than to assault LH181 with the limited force available. Of course, the more time we had available, the more the plan would improve, eventually reaching a state where, with Sheikh Mohammed's permission, we could implement it on a covert basis.

By now the quartermaster was really into the swing of things and the kit and equipment we needed was piling up: shotguns, masking tape, walkie-talkies, various ladders, padding and a myriad of other essential items. The commandeered Gulf Air 737 was now about to get the beating of its life, as I physically set about giving the team a crash course in anti-terrorist techniques. With the limited personnel and equipment available, it was no mean task.

On the personnel side, our resources were limited to a core of eight men who had received at least some professional CQB (Close Quarter Battle) training, and four who needed rapid training. Luckily, both Alastair and David Bullied were well trained as were the two Arab members of the Palace Guard – as the training progressed, the latter were quick to learn and displayed excellent qualities. Additionally, we discovered that the GSG9 members' experience in anti-terrorist techniques was equal to that of the SAS, and in certain areas better. For example, they had tried and tested all blind spots on various aircraft, and I was instructed to the millimetre just how much of a blind spot existed on the inner wing of a Boeing 737. At this stage every scrap of information would improve our chances of success. So I set about coaching my twelve good men, concentrating first on the immediate action drills needed to counter any anticipated terrorist deadline problems.

The Boeing 737 is a simple animal where anti-terrorist drills are concerned. There are only three possible places for entry: front and rear main doors, and the emergency exits over the wings. We were not aware at this time that all the passengers had been moved into economy-class accommodation, and that the terrorists had made the first-class compartment their office. Terrorists do not normally conduct their threats to governments while sitting amongst their hostages, so in LH181 they had to be in one of four places: in the small area at the rear of the aircraft by the rear doors and toilet; in the single aisle; around the catering area and front doors; or on the flight deck.

Armed with this information, and with our limited manpower, I based my assault plan on entry to the middle of the aircraft, via the over-wing emergency hatches. My thoughts were that if the terrorists began to carry out their threatened shootings, they would naturally take the precaution of covering the main doors. It seemed less likely that they would cover the two emergency exits.

Another important factor is that the wing emergency exits are designed to be opened easily from the outside, which is why I favoured this method of entry. The GSG9 had told me all about the blind spot; by placing a ladder gently against the trailing edge of the wing and as close as possible to the fuselage, it would be possible for two men to climb up and conceal themselves below the emergency hatch. From here it would be a simple matter of standing up and punching the small release panel on the hatch in order to force the hatch inwards. Anyone looking down from the aircraft windows would not see anything until the first man stood up. In the case of LH181, we had the additional advantage of the blinds being drawn.

The normal entry and exit points, front and rear, require considerable manhandling, and opening requires specialist training by anti-hijack teams working together. The front door is operable through a small hatch on the outside of the aircraft which allows the door to be opened and brought down automatically; a set of steps comes out at the same time. The problem with this operation is that it takes one and a half minutes before entry can be made to the aircraft. Basically, all the normal entry doors can be reached from the ground by short ladders – but a two-handed lever must be turned anti-clockwise in order to release the door, which then requires some effort to swing it open.

Once I had explained to the team the problems that faced us, I allocated people for the various positions. It was vital that Alastair and I plus two GSG9 personnel should go into the aircraft first. The basic common sense behind this decision is that we had trained for several years for just such a contingency, and this preparation would grant us the desperately needed edge. Just as critical to the operation is the immediate back-up, in case those going in first are killed – the assault would still need to be sustained. Once the assault was initiated, we would have no choice but to continue until the terrorists were neutralised.

Then I set about marking the area around the aircraft and the surrounding tarmac with chalk circles. It takes months even for trained professionals to adapt to the rapidly changing problems of assaulting an aircraft, and I had only a few hours in which to train everyone to move to the correct circle at the exact time.

The basic moves involved in the immediate action plan were:

(1) To make a single-file approach to the aircraft towards its blind spot at the rear. Once underneath the aircraft, we would quietly assemble our ladders and place them against the wings and the rear door

(2) To position four men from the leading assault teams covertly on the wings, one pair outside the port emergency exit, the other pair by the starboard exit. The back-up assault pairs would be waiting on the top rungs of the ladders, ready to follow the first pair in. Each of these assault teams consisted of either an SAS officer or a member of the GSG9, backed up by the best of the soldiers from the Palace Guard. We originally involved the Palace Guard in this part of the assault for purely political reasons, calculating that Sheikh Mohammed would favour us if we were willing to use his own countrymen. In the event they turned out to be very professional soldiers.

(3) To position an assault squad at the rear area of the plane by the port door, ready to scale their ladder, open the rear door and effect their entry as quickly as possible. At the same time, a second assault squad would be positioned beneath the front port door area, ready to erect their ladders and follow suit. The back-up personnel outside the aircraft would co-ordinate their moves with the progress of the assault teams.

(4) With everyone in position, and the command given, the leading assault teams were to stand, punch the emergency exit panels and drop the hatches into the laps of the passengers in the mid-section of the cabin. Each leading member would then throw stun grenades, one forward and one rear – this diversion would give us vital seconds during the assault. These teams would then enter, the port-side pair clearing forwards to the front and the flight deck, the starboard team clearing to the rear. The leading teams were to receive immediate back-up from the second assault pairs, entering behind them from their stations at the tops of the ladders. They would maintain

control of the centre of the aircraft or move down the aisle to assist the first groups if required.

(5) Simultaneously with the assault, the outside squads were to open both front and rear doors but not enter the aircraft, unless totally necessary. The intention was to provide further back-up in case of problems and also provide routes for the hostages to exit the aircraft, which by this time would be full of smoke from the stun grenades.

Once entry had been effected to the centre of the 737, the starboard assault team would gain a clear line of sight to the toilet doors at the rear of the cabin. The port team, moving forward through the economy area, would arrive in the first-class section, which in these aircraft leads into the front catering area. Directly beyond this is the flight deck, the door to which is usually closed. The only obstacles the team would encounter would be this door and the curtains in the catering and first-class areas. The door itself is light construction and easily removed by a solid push, so they would gain good coverage to the flight deck area.

Although this basic plan was quite uncomplicated, timing would be everything. I felt that a great deal of practice would be needed to get the timing correct, particularly the timing for the lead assault teams to effect their entry and take control of the front and rear aisle areas. I was conscious that, once we were in control of the aisle where all the passengers were seated, the only people in serious danger would be those on the flight deck.

To increase our chances of success and enhance the effect of the stun grenades, I had instructed one of the European seconded officers how to switch the APU on and off. He was to trip the switch the moment we stood to open the hatches, which would kill the lights, then three seconds after he heard the stun grenades going off he was to switch them on again. I hoped that by this time I would be in the aisle and closing rapidly with any terrorists at the front of the aircraft.

So at 8am on the 16th, sixty-five hours after LH181 had left Palma, the training and practice manoeuvres began. On command, members of the assault team moved on to their chalked positions in the manner required by the details of the operation. The necessary kit and equipment were brought into play as the practice continued, although at this stage we decided not to use the radios as they might give away our intentions. All morning we refined the basic plan, which was enhanced with many new ideas coming from Ulrich Wegener. By midday a lot of small snags had been sorted out and everyone was beginning to get the feel of the operation. The major priorities were that each person should know his own moves in the overall plan and also where everybody else was – the last thing I wanted was to shoot our own men. When we took our lunch break we made it a working one, using the time to iron out tiny details and searching constantly for anything that might increase the odds to our advantage.

One thing that improved those odds were the local soldiers from the Palace Guards. Initially involved only to ease diplomatic relations, they now exhibited their true value. They turned out to be extremely tough and very quick-witted, and could be relied on to do exactly as they were told in what was, for them, an entirely new kind of situation.

During our training Sheikh Mohammed left his diligent watch in the control tower and came to check what progress we were making. We went through our assault operation on the borrowed Gulf Air 737, and even at that early stage it looked pretty impressive and we were more or less ready to go should shooting break out.

Both Alastair and I firmly believed that, under cover of darkness, we could approach the hijacked aircraft and establish ourselves undetected. Once in our assigned starting positions, and given that we could put two four-men assault teams inside LH181, using the APU-powered lights plus the stun grenades as cover, there was a 99 per cent chance that we could close with the terrorists and eliminate them.

Despite our own state of readiness, however, there were still a number of factors beyond our control which quietly worried me. First among these was the location of the passengers. Would they be sitting down? Would some of them be in the aisle? The rapid clearing of the main aisle played a big part in our plan, for on it depended our ability to take command of the vital areas of the aircraft. I felt quite confident that, providing no one got in our way, we could kill the terrorists while minimising injury and loss of life to passengers and crew. But if our speedy progress was impeded the outcome might not be so good.

Another major concern was the state of the aircraft – suppose, for example, the terrorists had rigged LH181 with explosives? And what if they had grenades on board? But all these were imponderables and, without any hard evidence one way or the other, all we could do was our best.

For myself, I had no fear of the terrorists on LH181 – that is not conceit, it's just that I knew my own capabilities and I had total confidence in the training I had undertaken. Added to this, I had just spent several years fighting in far more dangerous conditions during the Oman War. In the early years of this conflict there were a lot of close engagements – not against a few people with a couple of pistols and some grenades as now, but against hard professional fighters. In some of those conflicts the weight of firepower against us was horrendous, and the air was thick with the singing of copper-coated bullets.

Our assault plan would be greatly enhanced by deploying suitable tactics to ensure that the hijackers were in given areas, for example standing in the catering areas looking down the aisles. This seemed to have been the standard position for terrorists on most previous Boeing 737 hijackings. If this can be achieved, an unexpected entry into the aircraft has a greater chance of success. During negotiations, talking to the terrorists or making them carry out some particular action can manoeuvre them to a specific location.

It is a misconception that when a hijacked aircraft is assaulted the terrorists start shooting their hostages. As soon as assault teams gain a standing position inside an aircraft and begin their back-to-back clearing up and down the aisles, the balance of power changes. Despite the terrorists' dedication and possible suicidal tendencies, once they have no hostages their very existence is under threat from the highly trained invaders. For maximum psychological advantage, these men are dressed to look evil, and they are armed with the most sophisticated weaponry that money can buy. They advance rapidly towards the terrorists with the sole aim of blasting their brains out. Fear makes terrorists' survival instinct come to the fore, and shooting hostages does not help in this situation. A terrorist's instinctive first action is to stop the invading beast bearing down on him. It takes only micro-seconds to choose between resistance or surrender, but he will be dead before he ever makes that choice.

After we had refined the assault plan, we started work developing external strategy such as diversions, an outer cordon and immediate medical assistance. All these preparations are as important as the assault itself. In the event of explosions, fire and casualties, we would need to have firm contingency plans.

Believing that we had the rest of the afternoon for further practice on the commandeered Gulf Air 737, we took another short break. I now felt reasonably satisfied that our ad hoc team had a workable structure and would respond well in the event of any immediate action required against LH181. For the moment the situation seemed stable, but as the 3pm deadline crept closer, there was an increased risk that the hijackers might start shooting hostages.

On board LH181, Mahmud realised that he was getting

nowhere fast with the approaching deadline and resumed his dialogue with Sheikh Mohammed. In the end, faced with a very serious threat from Mahmud to shoot several hostages, the Sheikh relented and sent out a truck to refuel the aircraft. He had been a skilful and patient negotiator, and he allowed a small quantity of fuel to be sent out to the stricken plane for humanitarian reasons so that the APU could continue to run. But he did not tell us of this, and it was about to cause a major shift in our planning.

Ulrich Wegener, Alastair Morrison and I were fairly confident that, given the go-ahead by Sheikh Mohammed, we could attack the aircraft that night. At about 2pm Alastair set off for the control tower to bring the Sheikh up to date with arrangements and to seek his permission. He succeeded, although there were a few slight disagreements, such as when Sheikh Mohammed wanted to block the runway to prevent the aircraft taking off. Alastair immediately advised against such an action, which might have caused Mahmud – already in a highly strung state – to make some drastic response.

But while Alastair and the Sheikh were discussing medical arrangements and other details they were suddenly interrupted by the speaker system in the control tower. Without warning, Mahmud's voice screamed out: 'We're taking off! We're taking off!' To everyone's horror, flight LH181 started to taxi down the runway, slowly gathering speed and lifting off into the clear blue Arabian sky.

As Dubai airport was still open, those of us that remained in the practise area were unaware that the aircraft taking off was indeed flight LH181. When, after a few minutes, Alastair returned and gave us the devastating information, there was a great deal of frustration and disappointment, as everything we had prepared and perfected so hurriedly and in such a short time had now gone to waste.

Sitting on the hot concrete, in the shadow of the wing of the Gulf Air 737, our group, which until a few moments ago had acted with a single dedicated purpose, was now decidedly sombre. Despite the short period of working together, a certain amount of camaraderie had developed, moulding the various nations of the ad hoc team together. We had worked hard, preparing for our assault on the aircraft, and now it was time to go our separate ways. Understandably, there was a certain amount of despondency amongst all concerned. The group broke up.

As the German negotiating team, consisting of Minister Wischnewski, Ulrich Wegener and the rest of the GSG9, went off to make their future plans and communicate the latest happenings to Germany, Alastair and I said our goodbyes to David Bullied and thanked everyone for their immense help and co-operation. I had never personally met David Bullied before, but I must say his exceptional qualities and involvement at Dubai have never been fully accredited to him.

14

THE BEASTS FROM HELL GET THEIR CHANCE

Having got to such a pitch of readiness and expectation we were all deeply disappointed and frustrated. What to do now? Alastair made contact with the British Consulate in Dubai, who had only just received information of our presence and were totally unaware of what had been happening. The Consul's wife very kindly organised food and asked if there was anything else they could do for us.

I had not had a bath for the past sixty hours and in the heat of the Middle East this was no fun for anyone. No sooner asked than granted. I was shown into a very luxurious bathroom and asked if I would like anything to drink. Now the SAS may be a tough outfit but I can be as decadent as the next man, and there is nothing finer than sitting in a tub of hot water whilst sipping a gin and tonic!

About five minutes later, as I lay soaking, there was a knock on the door and a very attractive lady brought in my drink on a silver tray. As she placed it down by the side of the bath, she looked at me and asked if there was anything else I would like. I desperately tried to position the sponge strategically – despite the setback with flight LH181, it seemed that luck had not entirely deserted me!

But just as I was about to reply Alastair came bounding up the stairs and informed me that we had to leave immediately. Is there no justice? It looked as if the game was back on: the GSG9 had requested our presence, and that of our stun grenades, on board the 707 negotiating plane, which was about to leave in hot pursuit of the hijacked LH181.

Back at the airport once more, we heard Minister Wischnewski reiterate what Alastair had already told me; then he asked if we felt we could join them for the next stage of the mission. Our brief from the Foreign Office had in fact been to go to Germany, and at most only as far as Dubai. But at times like this you turn a deaf ear to official instructions and make a decision on the spot. Of course we would go along with them.

About an hour later our Boeing 707 got airborne and we had an uneventful flight until we heard that the hijacked aircraft had landed in Aden – whether with permission or unannounced was not stated. We had thought at first that LH181 might try to land in Oman. This would have proved to our advantage, as there were anti-terrorist trained SAS soldiers stationed there. But even in Aden we would not be working on entirely unfamiliar ground. I was able to tell Ulrich Wegener that I knew Khormaksar Airport exceptionally well, and immediately started to make a drawing of the layout and to list other useful details.

Our pilot now radioed air traffic control in Aden, but was told in no uncertain terms that the runway was blocked and that no further aircraft were being allowed in or out. We had no option but to divert to Jiddah Airport in Saudi Arabia, where we eventually landed. Here we took advantage of the lull in proceedings to catch a couple of hours' sleep in the plane.

The energetic Minister Wischnewski, however, was hard at work again as soon as we landed. He went off to see officials of the Saudi government, in the hope of enlisting their aid in negotiations with their counterparts in Aden. At one stage, it seemed that the bargaining was going quite well and that the Saudis had managed to convince the Adenese government, and more importantly the hijackers, to release the hostages in exchange for the $15 million. Minister Wischnewski and the psychologist Wolfgang Salewski returned to our aircraft and informed us of this latest situation. However, one of the conditions was that all military personnel should immediately return to Germany.

I could see little reason for this – after all, we were at Jiddah Airport, hundreds of miles away from flight LH181. Nevertheless, Wischnewski insisted that all the GSG9 men, together with Alastair Morrison and myself, were to pack our equipment and leave on a small executive jet which was parked nearby.

As Alastair and I collected up our belongings, we became aware of an argument raging towards the front of the aircraft. Suddenly Wischnewski pushed the psychologist roughly aside and came storming down the aisle towards Ulrich Wegener, with whom he had a rapid discussion. Although we were not in earshot, it was obvious that some important matter had gone wrong. Wischnewski then came over to Alastair and me and switched to his perfect English. 'Gentlemen, I am sorry to mess you around, but there has been a major change of events. The pilot, Jürgen Schumann, has been shot dead in Aden. It is now our intention, and the intention of the German government, to follow flight LH181 wherever it may go and release the passengers.' Wischnewski was a tough character and had worked harder than anyone to release the hostages; the look on his face was one of sheer determination. Of course we would stay as long as required, and render whatever assistance we could.

Almost immediately, with renewed vigour, Ulrich Wegener and the GSG9 sergeant major sat down with Alastair and me at the rear of the aircraft and started discussing the possibilities of attacking the aircraft in Aden. I now produced the drawings of the airport that I had been working on from memory. But after about half an hour we were informed that the aircraft had left Aden and flown to Mogadishu in Somalia. Without further ado, Wishnewski ordered our own 707 negotiating aircraft to take off and we flew towards Mogadishu in the hope that we could finally assault the aircraft there.

During the flight, Wischnewski and the Bonn government applied all possible pressure to get permission to allow our aircraft to land in Mogadishu, and, they hoped, to receive some sort of political assistance there. A little over a year before, Mogadishu had been the base from which Wadi Haddad of the PFLP had directed the Entebbe operation. However, since that time there had been a major shift in Somali politics.

What appeared to have happened was that the LH181 had taken off from Dubai with insufficient fuel to go very far. Once it had reached its flying altitude the tanks were almost empty, and Jürgen Schumann had no choice other than to put the aircraft down or let it fall out of the sky. I believe at some stage he did consider ditching the aircraft in the Arabian Sea.

Omani air traffic control was working as normal, and received Schumann's first call at the Muscat control tower. Mahmud took the microphone from Schumann and said: 'Hello, hello, we're landing.' He repeated the phrase several times. The reply was short and to the point. 'You are refused landing – the airport has been blocked.' Mahmud then told Jürgen Vietor, who was at the controls, 'OK – take us to Aden.'

Schumann quickly worked out the distance and estimated their fuel requirements. 'We may just do it,' he said. He asked permission to move up to a height of 33,000 feet, the altitude which he considered most economical. Jürgen Vietor reset the plane's course and headed for Aden.

Once over Aden, Schumann spoke rapidly into the microphone: 'This is an emergency! We have no more fuel. We have no option but to either ditch into the sea or land. I am now making a descent into Aden Airport.'

As with everywhere else, the Adenese authorities refused permission.

Schumann immediately replied: 'I have ninety people on board. We will crash if you do not give us permission to land immediately.'

The Aden control tower replied: 'Stand by, stand by, we're checking.' After a few minutes another voice came back over the loudspeaker. 'I am sorry, the runway is blocked – there is no possibility of you landing here.'

Quickly checking his instruments, Schumann found that he had only fuel for, at best, twenty-five minutes flying time. The nearest airport was on the other side of the Red Sea in Djibouti, and there was absolutely no chance of making it. Jürgen Vietor took the aircraft down to 3,000 feet and passed over the airport, where he could vaguely make out the shapes of vehicles blocking the runway.

Schumann kept on talking to the control tower, announcing that they were coming into land irrespective of the blocked runway. He told the stewardesses to prepare the passengers for a crash landing. 'Everyone put your seats in the upright position, and heads down. Stand by to brace.' At an altitude of 500 feet Vietor put down the flaps, released the undercarriage and made his final approach.

'I'm going down to land in the sand,' said Vietor. 'Prepare for emergency landing. Extinguishers ready?'

'Extinguishers ready.'

'It's been a lovely life, but a bit short!' were Vietor's parting words to Schumann as he eased the aircraft down.

Seconds later the wheels touched the hard-packed sand

that ran parallel to the main runway. Using all his skill, Vietor brought the aircraft in and made a successful if bumpy landing. Once on the ground Captain Schumann requested Mahmud's permission to investigate the undercarriage to see if there had been any permanent damage which would affect the aircraft if it was required to take off again. He would also need to approach the control tower and request fuel.

Mahmud granted permission and Schumann left. After examining the undercarriage, and finding no serious damage, he made his way across to the control tower where he talked to the Adenese authorities. Whether he passed on any information at this stage is not known – he was certainly given a perfect opportunity. Mahmud began to get agitated about the length of time that Schumann had been away and yelled down the microphone to the control tower, informing them that unless Captain Schumann returned immediately to the plane he would execute some of the passengers. A few moments later, Schumann returned to the aircraft and a furious Mahmud ordered him to stand in the aisle.

Schumann's cool reserve had irritated Mahmud since the start of the hijack, and I feel that Mahmud saw the pilot as a serious threat to his authority on the aircraft. Mahmud thrust the pistol into Captain Schumann's face and shrieked: 'On your knees! On your knees! Hands on your head!' Schumann complied.

'I am going to hold a revolutionary tribunal. You have put us all in danger. You have been telling them all about our weapons and our explosives,' Mahmud challenged.

'No,' replied Schumann. 'I have been telling them about the aircraft and asking for fuel.'

'Liar! Are you guilty or not guilty?' shouted Mahmud, and slapped Schumann around the head.

'Please let me explain,' said Schumann.

'Liar!' thundered Mahmud again, hitting Schumann for a second time.

'If you will just let me explain . . .' But it was too late – Mahmud pushed the pistol directly into Schumann's face and pulled the trigger.

The blast reverberated around the cabin, its force smashing Schumann's body backwards so that it hit the side of the seats. Slowly he crumpled into the aisle. It all happened so abruptly, before mothers could cover the eyes of their children. For a moment there was a stunned silence, and then people started to whimper and cry. Rapidly, to support Mahmud, the other three hijackers started reasserting their position of authority by holding grenades up high and shouting for the passengers to keep quiet. Without a word, Mahmud turned and made his way to the flight deck. He picked up Schumann's hat, placed it on his head and sat in the pilot's seat.

Since the hijack, passengers have given various accounts of what happened to Schumann's remains. Some say his body remained lying where it had fallen in the aisle for at least two hours, so that people were forced to step over it on their way to the toilets. Others say that the second male hijacker and one of the passengers dragged the body to the rear of the aircraft and stuffed it in a cupboard there. What is known, however, is that when Jürgen Vietor landed the plane at Mogadishu the rear starboard door had been opened and the emergency chute inflated. Moments later, Schumann's body was thrown down the chute and landed in a heap on the tarmac. After negotiations with the control tower, the Mogadishu Airport Authority sent an ambulance across and removed the body of LH181's very courageous pilot.

Later, as emotional pressure mounted on the German government, the Pope volunteered to take the place of the hostages. In a message to the family of the murdered pilot, the Pope said: 'If it would be useful we would offer our own person for the liberation of the hostages. We appeal to the conscience of the hijackers, that they should refrain from this cruel undertaking.' LH181 was one of the very few hijacks in which the terrorists did not make a single concession.

Eventually our 707 negotiating aircraft took off from Jiddah in Saudi Arabia and flew south-west at low level towards Mogadishu. After about an hour, Alastair went forward to the flight deck and suggested putting look-outs at the windows, as well as keeping up continual radio dialogue to let any aircraft in the vicinity know that we were friendly. As Alastair pointed out, we were now flying over a major war zone, and Soviet fighters in the hands of either the Somalis or the Ethiopians might spot us on their radar and mis-identify us as hostile. This minor snippet of information drew looks of horror from the Germans, and immediately everyone was assigned to watch the windows like hawks for fighter aircraft.

As we approached Mogadishu Airport the loudspeaker broke into life, and we were told to fasten our seat belts and brace ourselves. Our pilot was about to approach the single runway with the intention of landing a short distance behind the hijacked aircraft. If he was successful, the terrorists would not realise that another German aircraft had landed.

As the pilot levelled the 707 for its final approach, we were only a few feet above the ground. The flat roofs of the airport buildings flashed underneath us as, with fantastic skill that bordered upon genius, the pilot managed to touch the aircraft down at the very edge of the runway. Weird screeching noises and smoke came from the undercarriage as the brakes were applied, bringing the giant aircraft rapidly to a halt. In the final seconds the pilot managed to turn our plane around and head back away from the hijacked aircraft. On board the 707 we all clapped.

We decided that all weapons belonging to the GSG9, Alastair and me, including the stun grenades, should be concealed from the Somali authorities. We were as yet unaware of their intentions or what sort of reception awaited us. So we stuffed everything into a catering trolley in the galley.

After a few minutes we were boarded by a Somali government reception party who, I was relieved to find, were both courteous and helpful. They were surprised to find two blue British documents amongst all the German green passports. When asked about this, Minister Wischnewski replied that we were two Middle East advisers who had been sent to help the Germans during this crisis. A few minutes later, the President of Somalia arrived.

President Siad Barre of the Somali Democratic Republic, as it was then known, was head of a state of 8 million inhabitants of one of the world's poorest and least-developed countries. Somalia has very few resources, and most of its economy is based on agriculture. Sadly, due to ever-increasing political turmoil there has been widespread famine.

The Somali government makes no territorial claims against any of its neighbours, but supports all legitimate rights of the ethnic Somalis of western Somalia and Eritrea. This was the basis of the Ogaden War that Alastair Morrison had warned the Germans about.

Earlier that year the Soviet Union, eager to acquire some influence in the Horn of Africa – the Americans were supporting Ethiopia – agreed to supply equipment to Somalia. But then President Carter suddenly stopped all aid to Ethiopia. Now, desperate for arms, that country turned to the Russians. The Soviet Union was happy to oblige, abandoning its previous commitment to Somalia. The war and the supply of war materials played a big part in the negotiations between President Barre and Minister Wischnewski. The hostages were about to become pawns in an even bigger political game.

Aboard the aircraft President Barre met Minister Wischnewski and shook hands with all of us. It was obvious now that the Somali government were well-disposed to the Germans and would help them in every way possible. I was later to learn that, after the Bonn government had been informed of flight LH181's arrival in Mogadishu, Chancellor Schmidt had spent an hour on the phone to President Barre.

As Wischnewski and the other members of the diplomatic team went off with President Barre, the rest of us were transferred by coach to the centre of Mogadishu, where we were booked into a big hotel. I decided it was about time that I had a change of clothing, but the best I could find lurking in my bag was crumpled, dirty and very smelly. So I ventured out in search of a pair of jeans and a tee-shirt.

Within a short distance I found what can loosely be described as a tailor's shop.

'Have you got any jeans and a tee-shirt?' I enquired in my best English.

The proprietor looked and sounded just like Manuel from *Fawlty Towers*, and clearly didn't have a clue. I pointed to the jeans and shirt I was wearing.

Manuel's eyes lit up and he dived under the counter, returning with a battered box that looked as if it had just done ten rounds with Mike Tyson. Proudly he opened the box to reveal a light green, short-sleeved Van Heusen shirt. Better still, it was actually my size.

'How much?' Now there's a phrase that's recognised in any language!

Manuel pointed to the battered box, which was marked '$15'. I nodded and pointed to my jeans in the hope that a pair of Levis might emerge from under that counter, but Manuel sadly shook his head. I paid him the $15 and returned to the hotel. Poor Manuel didn't look as if he'd eaten for weeks. To this day I still have that shirt. It's been washed so many times it looks like tissue paper, but I can't bring myself to throw it away.

Freshly showered and dressed in my nice clean shirt, I made

my way to the patio, where a large table had been lavishly spread for us, even in this poorest of poor countries. As we ate, the conversation drifted around the various current possibilities. The main priority at the moment was to extend the present deadline, which had now been set by Mahmud at 3pm that day.

A small team of German negotiators, including the psychologist Wolfgang Salewski, had been left at the airport and were continuing to talk to Mahmud. He had been categorically refusing to alter the deadline, but after some very delicate negotiation and a promise that the Baader-Meinhof were now being considered for release they managed to placate him. He eventually agreed to consider an extension. But this would be the final warning, Mahmud threatened. If his demands were not met then, the plane would be destroyed and all the hostages with it.

I truly think that at this stage Mahmud intended to destroy LH181 with explosives. Unknown to us, most of the male passengers had been tied up with tights and stockings taken from the women. Additionally, the terrorists had supposedly strapped explosives along the length of the main cabin – I say 'supposedly' because I checked the aircraft later and could find no evidence of this. Even so, they did empty all the duty-free alcohol along the aisle and under the seats – the stink and fumes almost knocked us sideways! If the terrorists did not wait too long, which would have enabled the alcohol to evaporate, the grenades would have set the aircraft alight.

My personal feeling is that Mahmud was at the end of his tether and was prepared to die on this operation – after all, from the outset he had referred to himself as 'Martyr Mahmud'. Whether his three colleagues felt the same is another story – but in any case five days is the average turning point in hijacks.

As we ate our meal in the hotel my attention was caught

by a young man of about thirty who went unnoticed by most of the Europeans, but attracted a lot of bowing and scraping from the locals. He must have been someone of importance as he strutted around with a very confident air. He circled our table a couple of times, eyeing us warily, and then noticed that I was watching him. Taking this as an invitation he came and sat down by me.

'Do you speak English?' He offered his hand.

'I am English.' I shook the hand.

'The President is going to allow the Germans to bring in their anti-terrorist team so they can free the hostages – Somalia is going to help.' Just like that he came out with it.

I just couldn't put my finger on it, but despite his smile he gave off a malevolence that I found disconcerting. 'That's great,' I said, 'but how do you know this – do you work for the government?'

'I am the deputy head of the security police.' He said it with great confidence – the same confidence that you get from pulling someone's fingernails out with a pair of pliers while extracting information. Still, what the hell – he was on my side! As the security guy and I continued our conversation about the hijack situation, a member of Wischnewski's team came out and informed us that the Somali government had agreed to our assault plan, and that the main bulk of the GSG9 team had now been given orders to fly to Mogadishu in preparation for the assult on the hijacked aircraft.

Immediately we collected our belongings from the hotel. Ulrich Wegener, Alastair Morrison, the GSG9 sergeant major and I crammed ourselves into a Somali jeep which was driven by no less than a Somali general, and swiftly we made our way to the airport.

Mogadishu Airport has two main entrances – one which goes to the passenger terminal, and one which leads around the back for domestic and service traffic. We drove to the latter. The airport, as expected, was heavily guarded by a ring of Somali troops. As our jeep approached the rear gate the general stopped the jeep some 50 metres short, even though we could plainly see a sentry standing at the barrier. Our general got out of the driving seat to identify himself, but instead of approaching the sentry he ducked down behind the jeep and shouted to him. If we weren't sure why he did this to start with, the next few moments put us right.

The sentry challenged again, this time pointing his AK47 machine gun at us. The Somali general shouted something back. Whatever he said it was wrong, for the sentry opened fire. The general leaped back into the driver's seat and we reversed rapidly. There then followed a rather farcical backwards and forwards dialogue as the general crept closer and closer to the sentry, assuring him that we were part of the German team. Eventually the general managed to reach the soldier and convinced him of his rank by beating him around the head several times.

From the control tower most of the negotiations with Mahmud were being conducted by the Somali Chief of Police, General Abdullah. Minister Wischnewski ordered that most of the conversation should be recorded by the co-pilot of our Boeing 707, Rüdiger von Lutzau. Rüdiger was the fiancé of Gaby Dillman, one of the stewardesses aboard flight LH181.

In the early stages of negotiation General Abdullah had tried hard to convince Mahmud that, if he released the hostages, he and his fellow terrorists would be given safe conduct. But Mahmud was having none of it – he thanked the Somali government for its offer but insisted as before that if his demands were not met by the time the deadline arrived he would destroy the aircraft. He even told the general he could watch the spectacular destruction of LH181 from the control tower.

Ulrich Wegener, Alastair Morrison and I then ran over the assault plan, which was based on the plan we had devised in Dubai, but now, since extra troops were available to us, would also incorporate the front and rear main doors. With a full team of GSG9 anti-terrorist trained personnel we stood an excellent chance of success.

The revised plan was fairly simple. The assault teams would leave the holding area and approach the hijacked aircraft from the rear, taking advantage of the blind spot which we already knew about. The men would approach the aircraft in a pre-arranged order and go to their assigned positions – these basically involved covering the two exit panels over the wings and opening the front and rear service doors.

The control tower would then need to keep up a continuous dialogue with the terrorists in the aircraft, confirming that the Baader-Meinhof terrorists had been released from German jails. The negotiators were to tell the terrorists that the aircraft had flown from Germany to Turkey to pick up the two additional PFLP terrorists. As our assault time approached, they were to say that it would be possible to talk to the released Baader-Meinhof prisoners using Lufthansa air-to-air communications.

It was vital that all this dialogue took place with Mahmud, because it would keep him on the flight deck. Any information on the terrorists' movements and location would be rapidly transmitted to the GSG9 commander positioned under the aircraft.

A diversionary fire would then be lit at the end of the runway, some 300 metres in front of the hijacked aircraft's nose. This could only be seen from the flight deck and would draw the terrorists' attention. It was, of course, essential that this fire was not lit a second too soon, or it would warn the terrorists that a strike was imminent. The task of creating this momentary diversion was given to the Somali general, to be carried out at Ulrich Wegener's command.

Seconds later, the 'Go' would be given and we would assault the aircraft. As the GSG9 made to open the doors,

Alastair and I would step away from the aircraft and throw our stun grenades. Ulrich Wegener decided that these grenades should not be used actually inside the plane, as his troops were not accustomed to fighting through the dramatic effect – word had clearly filtered down about the demonstration I had carried out at their HQ in Germany! Alastair and I were to throw one each over the wings, and another over the flight deck, which would have just as good an effect for our purposes. Fate must have been watching over us, as this decision was well made though for totally different reasons.

The Lufthansa Boeing 707 carrying the GSG9 men had originally been sent back to Bonn Airport from Turkey. However, the unit was still on stand-by and on Monday morning the aircraft took off and went to Crete, where it landed and refuelled, and then to Djibouti. As soon as Minister Wischnewski had obtained permission from President Barre of Somalia to use the GSG9, orders were sent for them to continue to Mogadishu.

As we waited for our reinforcements to arrive, the time was constructively spent carrying out a series of reconnaissance moves with particular attention to our intended approach route to the aircraft. During this recce we selected good concealment sites for the GSG9 snipers. The Somali Army had secured an exclusion zone around the immediate perimeter of the airfield; this was vital to the operation, as the German presence in Mogadishu was by now well known and it would have been simple for someone to signal to the terrorists. Mind you, if the rest of the Somali soldiers were anything like the one guarding the gate when we arrived, I pity any poor bastard who ventured even near the airport perimeter!

Back at the airport buildings we made arrangements for the collection of the hostages once they had been released. Unsure how it was all going to go, we decided we would guide them to the rear of the aircraft. Once the assault had proved successful, the snipers would come forward and take charge of the hostages until the ambulances arrived.

While we were preparing ourselves, the poor hostages were reaching the point of total despair. With the men tied up and the interior of the plane soused with highly inflammable spirits, they must have been certain that this would be their last day on earth. Sometime later stewardess Gaby Dillmann begged Mahmud for permission to speak to the tower. Unknown to her, her boyfriend Rüdiger von Lutzau was listening in just a few hundred metres away. Mahmud handed her the microphone.

'We know this is the end, and that we shall all die. Many of us are too young to die. Still, it is better to die than live in a world where human lives count for so little. I hope it will be quick. What is more important – to keep nine people in jail or save the lives of ninety? Tell my family it wasn't so bad, and please tell my boyfriend that I loved him very much.' There was a pause, then she said, 'I don't know what kind of people we have in our government – I only hope they can live with this on their consciences.'

As the day dragged on, the Somali general tried in vain to extend the afternoon deadline, but Mahmud flatly refused. Convinced that he was going to destroy the aircraft, the Somalis begged for an extra half hour to clear the area. Mahmud promised to consider it.

While he was still debating the request, the tower suddenly came back to him. 'This is the German chargé d'affaires. Can you hear me, Martyr Mahmud?'

'I hear you clearly. What does the representative of the fascist West German regime want?'

'We have news of the prisoners you wish to have released from German jails. They are to be flown to Mogadishu. However, due to the great distance and the fact that they have to stop at Turkey to pick up the two Palestinians, the aircraft cannot be here before tomorrow morning.'

Mahmud was not having it. 'You dare to ask me to extend the deadline until tomorrow? Why have the fascist German government waited until now?'

'I cannot answer that, but yes, I am asking you to extend the deadline,' replied the chargé d'affaires.

'What is the distance between Germany and Mogadishu?' Mahmud demanded.

'About seven thousand miles . . . I am not sure, I will check.'

'I will check also. Do not play games with me, fascist representative – if you are lying I will blow up the plane!'

Every word that was spoken was analysed by the German psychologist Wolfgang Salewski. At this stage it looked as if Mahmud had taken the bait. The distance and flight times had been worked out correctly, which was just as well – it would have been hard to bluff Mahmud at this point, as he had trained as an aeronautical engineer.

'We have worked out the route,' said the chargé d'affaires. 'It is approximately 3,960 nautical miles and will require a little over seven hours for the aircraft to fly here. We must also add to this the time required to pick up the two Palestinians from Turkey.'

Mahmud did not seen too happy about the extension, but faced with the alternative he agreed to extend the deadline to 01.30 European Standard Time the next morning. Back in the aircraft, Mahmud relayed the good news to the rest of the terrorists and the hostages. 'I have just spoken to the representative of the fascist German government. They have agreed to all our demands. I am going to set you all free.' Mahmud went back to the flight deck and spoke to the co-pilot, Jürgen Vietor. 'You have done your job. You are free to go.'

Vietor was stunned at this opportunity, but deep down he

knew he could not leave. 'I think I will stay,' he replied, 'if that's OK with you.'

Mahmud nodded and told Vietor to move into the first-class section, where he would be more comfortable.

At about eight o'clock that evening, the Lufthansa 707 carrying twenty-eight members of the GSG9 finally arrived at Mogadishu Airport. Almost immediately the troops started gathering their equipment together and dressing themselves ready for the assault. Ulrich Wegener assembled them with Alastair and me and briefed them, after which they separated into their various groups ready to prepare their equipment.

The snipers fitted 'owl's eye' night sights to their Mauser 66 sniper rifles. As soon as they were ready, Ulrich Wegener detailed them to their individual locations. Once in position around LH181 they could report back precise minute-by-minute information. The time was 22.05 hours GMT.

Most of the assault group were in civilian clothes – I had a notion that the Somali government were not too keen on having a uniformed foreign power carrying out a military action. However, as Alastair and I were not known to most of the team we were given spare GSG9 shirts from which all insignia had been removed, though the garments would still be recognisable to the Germans, who would therefore identify us as friend, not foe.

The assault teams put on their British-made body armour and fitted up their Heckler and Koch MP5 machine guns in exactly the same way as the SAS. However, it would appear that most of the first wave going into the aircraft would be using pistols. This may seem a little strange, but they first had to get through a small hatch where a larger weapon would be cumbersome, and in a confined space like an aircraft a pistol is more flexible. Not that I liked the Germans' choice of hand guns – they were using either small 9mm P9s or the Smith and Wesson .38 special revolver. Give me the

Browning 9mm Hi-Power every time – not only does it give you thirteen shots, but it tends to stop whatever you hit. It was interesting to note at this stage that the Germans were using two ladders strapped side by side for the main door entry points. This technique allowed the man on the left to operate the locking handle and open the door, leaving one man on the right immediate access to the aircraft.

At last everyone was ready, and a full dress rehearsal was conducted using the Lufthansa 707. It was soon clear that the drills adopted by the GSG9 were almost totally compatible with those of the SAS, right down to the equipment and method of approach and assault. We felt that as a team we were as finely tuned as we could possibly be.

At 23.00 hours standard European time, it was time to start for real. We formed a single column, and at about 23.30 the whole group assembled on the edge of the runway directly behind LH181. Having waited a few moments for the snipers to report the all-clear, we began to approach the aircraft from the rear. At this stage we were well concealed, since none of the aircraft windows looked in this direction. But when we were about 150 metres away from the aircraft, out on the smooth runway, we were horrified to discover that the airfield lights coming from the direction of the control tower were casting long shadows off us. The closer we got to the aircraft, the more chance there was of someone looking through a window and seeing the column of marching shadows. And the closer we were, the larger our shadows seemed to become. At one point they were some 25 feet long. We bent double to minimise the effect, but there was little else we could do. Luckily we reached the aircraft and fell under its shadow without being seen.

Immediately everyone went to his assigned position and we started erecting the assault ladders. This done, those by the wings crawled silently up the ladders and adopted their positions beneath the emergency hatches. It was vital that everyone kept tight into the body of the plane so that they could not be seen through the windows.

Alastair had been assigned the port side of the aircraft, and on the 'Go' command was to throw a stun grenade over the wing emergency exit. I was positioned on the starboard side and was to throw a grenade over the wing exit and a second one over the cockpit, in order to distract the terrorists as the assault team went in. After that, I was to assist the starboard wing assault teams.

For some reason there seemed to be a problem by the rear door where I was standing. The assault ladder had been adjusted to fit the 707 aircraft on which the GSG9 had practised, but this was a much smaller aircraft and consequently the assault ladders were far too long for the job in hand. They stuck out at an angle of 45 degrees and kept slipping down the rounded body of the fuselage. Ulrich Wegener, who was now crouched underneath the aircraft, quickly whispered into his radio. Quickly two medical personnel arrived from the rear of the aircraft and supported the ladder against the fuselage. This was no mean feat, due to the fact that two rather large GSG9 members were standing on the top of the ladder.

Ulrich Wegener was now in constant communication with the control tower. I crouched down near him to listen in as he pressed the earpiece close and listened intently to the whispered conversation. Then he turned to me and said, 'They have two men in the cockpit – they can hear them – and possibly one of the girls.'

At that time, the negotiators in the control tower were carrying out their role in the assault plan, convincing Mahmud that he had indeed won the day, and that the West German government had fully capitulated. The $15 million was already in Mogadishu and on board the negotiating plane, he was told, and at any time they requested this money it would be available. Additionally, the Germans had agreed to the release of all eleven Baader-Meinhof in German jails and they were now being flown to Mogadishu. The aircraft bringing the terrorists had called off in Turkey to pick up the two PFLP prisoners whose release had also been requested by Mahmud.

Without making any promises, the negotiating team told Mahmud that he could soon speak to the Baader-Meinhof people using air-to-air communication. The negotiators asked him to consider how he would like the exchange to take place once he had had this conversation.

As the climax drew nearer, the exchange between Mahmud and the control tower was almost non-stop. Every possible effort was being made to concentrate Mahmud's mind on anything other than the idea of the aircraft being attacked. The main topic of conversation was the exchange of hostages.

'There will be no reporters present at the exchange – is this understood?' Mahmud snapped.

'Understood.'

'No one is to approach the aircraft commanded by the Halimeh unit without permission – is that understood?'

'Understood.'

'When our comrades arrive you will send only one to us so that we can be sure of the rest – understood?'

'Understood.'

Mahmud was about to give his next instruction when a huge fireball leaped into the sky about three hundred metres in front of the aircraft. The Somali soldiers had lit their fire, as requested, to draw the attention of the hijackers. They must have set fire to a complete tanker full of petrol as the whole airfield was suddenly illuminated. Although all this grabbed Mahmud's attention, he did not appear to feel threatened by it. The other male terrorist, Abbasi, who was standing in the cockpit doorway, merely shrugged his shoulders. Undeterred, Mahmud continued: 'A member of the Somali . . .'

At that moment there was a blinding flash outside the cockpit window, followed by a deafening explosive shock-wave. Mahmud reeled and staggered backwards into his fellow terrorist. From his seat in the first-class section the co-pilot Jürgen Vietor also saw the flash and felt the thunder, and instantly put his head between his legs. The beast from hell was knocking on the door.

The last thing I heard Ulrich Wegener say was, 'Three, two one, GO!'

Instinctively I stepped away from the aircraft, having already pulled the pins from the two stun grenades which I was clutching. I tossed the first one casually in an arc over the starboard wing. It exploded about three feet above the two GSG9 soldiers waiting there, causing them great surprise! Just as it exploded, they punched in the panel which released the small hatchway into the aircraft. Taking a better swing, I threw the second grenade high over the cockpit. It actually exploded about two feet above the flight deck, to dramatic effect.

After throwing the second grenade, I whipped round to see the GSG9 soldier on my left turn the handle of the rear starboard door and with a kick throw his body clear of the ladder, still hanging on to the handle and pulling the door open on its hydraulics. The moment he did this the internal lights of the aircraft revealed one of the female terrorists standing there in a Che Guevara tee-shirt, wearing an expression of utter astonishment. At that instant the soldier on the right rung of the ladder fired a burst and stitched her with at least six rounds. She fell to the floor, dead, and the soldier disappeared into the aircraft.

Returning my attention to the starboard wing, I ran forward and scaled the small ladders, positioning myself by the open hatchway where the two GSG9 had already entered. As I looked into the aircraft I saw that the hatchway had fallen on the laps of the two passengers sitting there. They sat frozen, their eyes closed tightly. Continuous gunfire rattled up and down the aircraft for what seemed a lifetime. I can remember saying to myself, 'Come on, do it, do it – get it done!' Then came a couple of low thuds as two of the terrorists' grenades exploded.

After our stun grenades had gone off Abbasi was the first to move, trying hard to shake off the ringing effect in his ears. He almost made the first-class compartment, but Soraya was blocking his way. At first Abbasi could not understand it – Soraya seemed to be running into the toilet, someone was chasing her down the aisle. Then the door to his right opened. Abbasi never knew what hit him as he got caught in cross-fire. Mahmud watched as his colleague crumpled to the floor with over twenty bullets in him, then he too felt bullets ripping and burning through his body. He could not remember having pulled the pins from the grenades, but now they rolled out of his hands, forwards into the first-class section.

Vietor heard the first explosion. 'This is it,' he thought, 'I'm going to die.'

Gaby Dillmann sat in the aisle seat, her legs in the gangway. As the grenade exploded, a fragment of white-hot metal ripped into her calf muscle. She thought, 'It's only my legs – it doesn't hurt.' Then men were rushing past her, shooting towards the flight deck and shouting: 'Get down! Get down!'

In the chaos no one saw Soraya dive into the toilet, from where she now started to shoot. But instantly the fire was returned, and as the door burst open her body hit the floor.

The firefight by now had lasted some four or five minutes and was confined to the cockpit part of the aircraft, where sudden sharp bursts interspersed with single shots could still be heard. It was quite clear that the passengers had been strapped into their seats in the economy section, and would therefore be clear of any immediate danger. Cries of 'Get down! Get down!' from the GSG9 continued to echo around the aircraft as they fought the remaining terrorists. Then, out of the rear starboard door, I saw figures start to appear and descend the assault ladders. One of the GSG9 soldiers pulled the hatchway off the laps of the couple who had been trapped and at last they opened their eyes; I reached in to help them out of the aircraft. The exodus continued smoothly as more and more people disembarked. Once on the tarmac they were guided towards the rear of the aircraft where they assembled, waiting for the stream of ambulances and buses now making their way across from the main terminal buildings.

I climbed down and went round to the port side, where I found Alastair Morrison. He was helping a young lady climb down off the wing, catching her in his cradled arms. She looked like one of the eleven beauty queens. 'You'll have to give her back!' I warned him. Alastair insisted on carrying her to safety at the rear of the aircraft.

Suddenly, shouting broke out on the port wing and I looked up to see a man crouched by the emergency hatchway over the wing, with the GSG9 shouting: 'Come down! Come down!' He refused and, reaching back into the aircraft, he dragged out a small boy who turned out to be his son. Of all the incidents that night, this was one of the few things I remember clearly. It was a simple action, but when you consider the situation – fear that the aircraft might explode at any moment, people around you screaming, soldiers shouting commands – an action like that takes great courage.

Leaving Alastair to his beauty queen, I went round to the starboard side to check on progress. Suddenly the GSG9 sergeant major stood up in the rear doorway and shouted: 'They're all out, they're all free!'

Climbing back on to the wing, I re-entered the aircraft via the emergency hatch. Strangely, as if this Boeing 737 was a living thing, it seemed tired, like a hunted fox. Exhausted and hurt, it now sat quietly resting. The first thing that struck me was the stink – alcohol fumes mixed with urine bleached the air. In this unreal silence I saw Alastair coming up the aisle from the rear door. Together we went on to the flight deck, where we found Ulrich Wegener, still with a gun in his hand, and the Somali general. I was surprised to find a fairly heated conversation taking place between the two men. The subject seemed to be the bodies of the terrorists that lay at their feet. Mahmud appeared to be still alive, as did one of the women. It was eventually agreed that these two should be removed from the aircraft and taken to the airport terminal building for medical attention.

As the female terrorist was placed on a stretcher she defiantly showed everyone that she was not dead. 'Kill me, kill me!' she shouted, before raising her right hand, giving the V for victory sign and screaming several times: 'Free Palestine, free Palestine!' But Mahmud was in a very serious condition and there was no doubt that he would not make it for more than a few hours. Indeed, he died later in hospital.

Once the assault was over, everyone was quickly checked for injuries sustained during the rescue attempt. One member of the GSG9 had been hit, and Gaby Dillmann had shrapnel in her leg, but luckily both these were fairly minor injuries and they were able to return to Germany straightaway.

In the crowded airport lounge passengers were wandering around, still unable to believe that they were free. Despite the traumatic conditions the place was fairly quiet, with most of the noise coming from the surviving female terrorist. Then I saw the man who had reached back into the aircraft for the little boy. He stood still holding the child, his eyes red with fatigue, while a young woman hugged him and rested her head on his shoulder. In another corner, Gaby Dillmann, quite unaware until now that her fiancé had volunteered to fly one of the Boeing 707s to Mogadishu, was being fussed over by him. I believe that as they sat there reunited in the airport lounge, Rudeger proposed and they are now happily married. The rest of the freed hostages just looked absolutely exhausted, their hair wildly unkempt and their clothes all stained and dirty – but they were alive.

Within the hour it was decided that all the rescued passengers would be put on board the negotiating aircraft on which we had arrived, and that Alastair Morrison, Wegener and I would return with the GSG9 on their Boeing 707. The hijacked 737 was to remain where it stood for the moment. Poor old LH181 was looking a bit sad.

While all this was going on, Minister Wischnewski was in contact with Chancellor Schmidt from the control tower. Immediately the assault had been confirmed as successful, at 12.08, Minister Wischnewski radioed Bonn with the news. 'Tell the world Germany has done it, the job's done,' he said.

15

END OF THE BAADER-MEINHOF

The announcement was made on German Radio half an hour after midnight on Tuesday, 18 October. Insomniacs' ears pricked up as a news flash was announced. A newscaster came on to say that all eighty-six hostages had been safely freed, three terrorists killed and the fourth seriously injured.

As we got ready to depart, Alastair and I sat there quietly congratulating ourselves on our small part in this rescue assault. But even now we could not afford to relax completely. Alastair suggested to Ulrich Wegener that he should put a small group of GSG9 soldiers on the Boeing 707 carrying the rescued passengers home. The reason, he explained, was that there might be sleepers amongst the passengers. Sleepers are people who remain on the aircraft but are actually part of the hijack plan, so that once the aircraft has taken off again the same scenario can be repeated if these people have weapons. So, as a precaution, there was now a delay of fifteen minutes while the GSG9 rapidly unpacked some of their weapons from the hold and went across to board the 707 carrying the passengers.

At about 3.15am, both aircraft took off for Germany. Once we had reached our cruising height there was much to celebrate. The Lufthansa crew were happily breaking out copious quantities of duty-free and dispensing it to the GSG9 troops and ourselves. But unfortunately there was little food on board, and I was starving.

In a demob-happy party spirit we told a lot of jokes, most of which were unprintable. Then someone suggested we should play cards, using the ransom money. This ransom money had been with Alastair and me since we first left Germany for Dubai. It was contained in a desk-sized aluminium suitcase that required at least four people to carry it. There was no risk that anyone would steal it, and for most of the time it had sat unattended on the back seat of the negotiating aircraft.

That day, 18 October, the London *Times* received the following letter. The envelope was postmarked from Mainz in West Germany and bore the date of 14 October. Enclosed with the letter was an 'ultimatum' addressed to 'The Chancellor of the Federal Republic of West Germany'. It was dated 13 October.

> *Communiqué.*
> Operation Kofr Kaddum.
> To all revolutionaries in the world.
> To all free Arabs.
> To our Palestinian masses.
>
> Today, Thursday, 13 October 1977, the Lufthansa 737 plane leaving from Palma to Frankfurt, flight number 181, has come under the complete control of our 'Martyr Halimeh' commando unit. This operation aims to free our comrades from the prisons of the imperialist-reactionary-Zionist alliance. This operation emphasises the aims and the demands of the 'Siegfried Hausner' commando unit operation of the RAF (Rote Armee Fraktion) that began on 5 September 1977.

Revolutionaries and freedom fighters all over the world are confronted with the monster of world imperialism, the barbarous war, the hegemony of the USA against the people of the world.

In this war imperialist sub-centres as the Zionist entity and West Germany have the executive function of oppressing and liquidating revolutionary movements in their specific areas.

In our occupied land the imperialist Zionist, reactionary enemy demonstrated the highest level of its bloody hostility and aggressively against our people and revolution, against all the Arab masses and their patriotic and progressive forces. The expansionist and racist nature of the Zionist entity – with Menachem Begin on top of this product of imperialist interests – clearer than ever before.

On the same imperialist interests West Germany was built up in 1945 as a US base. Its function is the reactionary integration of the Western European countries by economic oppression and blackmail. As far as the underdeveloped countries of the world are concerned, West Germany is giving financial, technical and military support to the reactionary regimes in Tel Aviv, Teheran, Pretoria, Salisbury, Brasilia, Santiago de Chile, etc.

Between the two regimes in Bonn and Tel Aviv there is a close and special co-operation going on in military and economic field, as well as in common political positions. The two hostile regimes are jointly facing the patriotic and revolutionary movements of liberation in the world in general and in the Arab area, Africa and Latin America in particular. Both regimes actively participate in every attempt of liquidating armed struggle in Africa. This is manifested by their supply of the minority racist regimes atomic know-how, by delivering them mercenaries and credits, by opening markets for their products, by breaking the boycott and economic siege around them.

A significant example of the close co-operation between Mossad and the German intelligence service, together with the CIA and DST, was the dirtiest piracy of the imperialist, reactionary alliance: the Zionist invasion of Entebbe.

Actually the similar character of neo-Nazism in West Germany and Zionism in Israel is getting ever clearer, too. In both countries reactionary ideology is dominant; fascist, discriminatory and racist labour laws are enforced; the ugliest method of psychological and physical torture and murder are applied against fighters for freedom and national jubilation; forms of collective punishment are practised; all provisions of international law as to the rights of detainees for human treatment, just trial and defence are completely abolished.

While the Zionist regime is the most genuine and practical continuation of Nazism, the Bonn Government and the parties of its parliament are doing their best to renew Nazism and expansionist racism in West Germany, particularly in the military establishment and other state institutions.

The economic circles and the magnates of the multinational companies in West Germany play an effective role in these efforts. Ponto, Schleyer and Buback are mere examples of persons who have well served old Nazism and are now practically executing the aims of the new Nazis in Bonn and the Zionists in Tel Aviv – both locally and internationally.

One part of these enemies' anti-guerrilla strategy is the non-compliance with the legitimate demands for setting free our detained revolutionaries, who suffer the most cruel forms of torture with the silent knowing of the international public. We declare that this doctrine will not succeed. We will force the enemy to free our prisoners who daily challenge him by going on to fight oppression even in jail.

Victory to the unity of all Revolutionary Forces in the World.

Struggle Against World Imperialism Organisation, SAWI0. 13.10.1977

Ultimatum
to the Chancellor of the
Federal Republic of West Germany

This is to inform you that the passengers and the crew of the Lufthansa 737 plane, flight no. 181 leaving from Palma to Frankfurt, are under our complete control and responsibility. The lives of the passengers and the crew of the plane, as well as the life of Dr Hans-Martin Schleyer, depend on your fulfilling the following.

1. Release the following comrades of the RAF (Rote Armee Fraktion) from prisons in West Germany – Andreas Baader, Gudrun Ensslin, Jan-Karl Raspe, Verena Becker, Werner Hoppe, Karl-Heins Dellwo, Hanna Krabbe, Bernd Rossner, Ingrid Schubert, Irmgard Moller, Gunter Sonnenberg and with each the amount of DM100,000.

2. Release the following Palestinian comrades of PFLP from prison in Istanbul-Mahdi and Hussein.

3. The payment of the sum of $15m according to accompanying instructions.

4. Arrange with any one of the following countries to accept to receive all the comrades released from prison: 1) Democratic Republic of Vietnam; 2) Republic of Somalia; 3) People's Democratic Republic of Yemen.

5. The German prisoners should be transported by plane, which you should provide, to their point of destination. They should fly via Istanbul to take in the two Palestinian comrades released from Istanbul prison. The Turkish Government is well informed about our demands.

The prisoners should all together reach their point of destination before Sunday 16th of October, 1977,

8.00am (GMT). The money should be delivered according to accompanying instructions within the same period of time.

6. If all the prisoners are not released and do not reach their point of destination, and the money is not delivered according to instructions, within the specified time, then Dr Hans-Martin Schleyer, and all the passengers and the crew of the Lufthansa 737 plane flight no. 181, will be killed immediately.

7. If you comply with our instructions all of them will be released.

8. We shall not contact you again. This is our last contact with you. You are completely to blame for any error or fault in the release of the above mentioned comrades in prison or in the delivery of the specified ransom according to the specified instructions.

9. Any try on your part to delay or deceive us will mean immediate ending of the ultimatum and execution of Dr Hans-Martin Schleyer and all the passengers and the crew of the plane.

There is no doubt that whoever wrote this letter to *The Times* also wrote the original demand note that was sent to the Protestant Dean of Wiesbaden. The letter was posted in Mainz, and Wiesbaden is only just down the road – not only that, the order in which the Baader-Meinhof names appear is the same.

But now it was all too late – both for the Baader-Meinhof prisoners and for their last victim, Hans-Martin Schleyer.

As the exhilarated, exhausted crew, passengers and their hero rescuers flew home, several thousand miles away in Stammheim jail, Stuttgart, prison officers discovered several members of the Baader-Meinhof gang dead or dying. Even before the celebrations started, West Germany would become very aware of the rapid change in the state of play and the position in which these suicides would place the government.

Of the four people who had attempted suicide, three now lay dead, with the survivor in hospital. The same three also happened to be the main players in the terrorists' demands. Had the hijackers succeeded in their demands Andreas Baader Gudrun Ensslin, Jan-Karl Raspe and Irmgard Moller would have been flying towards a Communist country that had agreed to provide them with refuge, and they would have been better off to the tune of $15 million.

At 9am that day, Chancellor Helmut Schmidt was at home celebrating the success at Mogadishu when he was told of the deaths of the prisoners. He was absolutely stunned. Just as the government were congratulating themselves on the success of the hijacking situation and beginning to relax, here was yet another blow to their credibility and another huge media story that would need careful handling, for the deaths would arouse suspicion.

During the previous four days the Baader-Meinhof prisoners had begun to appreciate their ability to gain the immediate attention of any official of whatever rank. Now, after the events at Mogadishu, they would have very little control over their future. During the night of 17–18 October the situation at the prison seemed normal. There were no reports of any disturbance, and as most of the prisoners on the seventh floor had, as usual, taken some sort of sedative, none was expected.

Stammheim is no ordinary prison. It is a very modern maximum-security prison, specially built to house such criminals as the Baader-Meinhof. The seventh floor, where the suicides occurred, is the top floor. The roof above is designed to prevent not only escape but also any potential rescue by helicopter. The seventh floor itself is divided by a wide corridor, with five cells on one side and three on the other. At the end of the corridor is a permanently manned guard room. From this room, which controls the only access, the corridor can be observed through bullet-proof glass which allows the guard to see every cell door.

On the left, the side with three cells, Baader and Raspe were housed, with Raspe closest to the guard. There was an empty cell between the two. On the other side were housed Ensslin and Moller, with Moller being closest to the guard. Once again an unused cell divided the two women.

Although after the kidnapping of Hans-Martin Schleyer the cells had been padded to prevent any contact between the terrorists, they could still shout from the top floor and be heard in the street. This is verified by several reporters who clearly heard them while waiting outside the prison. Additionally, after the suicides all the inmates of the prison were questioned. Several from the floor below said the only thing they heard was Baader and the others walking about or going to the toilet. But Raspe and Baader died by shooting, and no one heard any shots.

Early next morning, as the night shift handed over to the day shift, there was nothing unusual to report. The normal routine started, which mainly involved passing keys to each other, waking the prisoners and preparing breakfast. Before the occupant of each cell could be released, padding that covered his or her door to prevent the gang communicating during the night had to be removed. By the time this had been carried out on Raspe's cell it was just past 7.30am. The staff had released the central locking system to the cells and expected to be greeted as usual on their breakfast round by the prisoners standing by their cell doors. The fact that Raspe did not appear at his door set off mental warning bells. Immediately the officers congregated at his cell. Looking in, they saw everything in disarray and what appeared to be Raspe's body lying across his bed with his head turned away, falling forward on his chest. There was blood on his head and on the wall next to him. Raspe was still breathing. The cell door was immediately locked. Officers went quickly to the phone to ring the doctor and call for medical orderlies. This was all done very discreetly so as not to alert the other occupants of the floor.

When the officers and the medics arrived they found Raspe still alive and also noticed a pistol in the cell. Reports made afterwards do not state where exactly the pistol was found. The gun had been picked up and wrapped in a piece of cloth, which would surely have wiped off any fingerprints or blood.

Was the gun taken from Raspe's hand? Was it taken from the floor or the bed? When and if it was removed from his hand, had it been loose in his hand or was he gripping the gun? Was it in his left hand or his right hand? Did the patient show any signs of shooting himself when he was first seen by the medical orderlies? This, remember, was 1977, with sophisticated methods of discovering and assessing forensic evidence. The Baader-Meinhof were also a volatile group of prisoners with a very high media profile.

An ambulance arrived at about 8am and Raspe was taken to hospital, where he was given emergency treatment and X-rayed and prepared for theatre. But to no avail. He died at 9.40am.

After Raspe's ambulance had left the prison, the guards returned to their normal routine of taking breakfast to the other prisoners. At about ten past eight the door of Baader's cell was opened after they had removed the soundproof padding. When the officers opened his door there was a mattress blocking their view. They pushed the mattress out of the way and went in. The curtains were drawn and the room was dark. In the dim light the medical orderly, who had stayed with the officers, saw Baader lying on the floor with his head in a pool of blood. The medic felt for signs of life – there were none. A gun lay beside the body and this was noticed by one of the prison officers. They locked the cell door, but since there was no point in calling the doctor again they quickly went to the other cells and started to unlock them.

In Gudrun Ensslin's cell they again had to remove a screen and go into an ill-lit room. They saw two feet hanging from the cell window. When the prison doctor came he confirmed that this prisoner too was dead – though the post-mortem does not seem to record time of death for either Baader or Ensslin.

The prison officers and medical staff must have positively rushed to Irmgard Moller's cell, where they found her lying on her bed covered by a blanket. The orderly turned her over, probably expecting to find yet another corpse. But as he removed the blanket she moved and groaned. There was blood on her, which made the orderly suspect that she had cut her wrists. Yet when he examined her hands he could see no signs of injury. Examining her further, he discovered that she had wounds on her chest. Her vital signs, however, appeared strong and she also seemed to be conscious. The prison doctor treated her for heart failure and covered her wounds, after which she was immediately taken by ambulance to a different hospital from the one which had received Jan-Karl Raspe. Later she was operated on to repair damage to her heart caused by puncturing the pericardium – the sac around the heart. But nobody commits suicide this way – why didn't she just cut her wrists? And after she had stabbed herself, would she really cover herself with a blanket?

In the days immediately before these traumatic events the four had several times spoken to government officials and their prison warders. Ensslin and Baader had demanded that members of the crisis committee, originally set up because of Hans-Martin Schleyer's kidnapping, should come and talk with them. Two people were to comply with their request.

The first was Assistant Minister Dr Hegelau, who had never met Baader; Alfred Klaus, who knew Baader well, was to accompany him. While they were waiting to talk to Baader, they heard Gudrun Ensslin make a request for contact with two prison chaplains, who were helping the four relieve the psychological stress of the no-contact order.

When Hegelau and Klaus finally spoke with Baader, he discussed the alternatives left for the government and himself over the hijack hostage situation. Andreas Baader discussed the purpose of the Red Army Faction and the point of their involvement. He is believed to have said that the prisoners would have to die one way or another.

The same afternoon Gudrun Ensslin spoke to two chaplains, one a Protestant and the other a Catholic. She asked that in the event of her death they should pass on to her lawyer three letters written by her and kept in a file in her cell. She implied during the conversation that she might not live much longer. The chaplains told the prison authorities of this conversation, and discussed whether she had meant execution or suicide. After her death, of course, there appeared to be no evidence of this file or the three letters. But why did she think at this stage that she might die? The hijack was still in full swing, and Schleyer was still a captive. What had made her and Baader think like this?

On 17 October the prisoners had had no contact with the outside world since 5 September. As a last resort Baader's defence lawyer, Hans Heldman, tried ringing Amnesty International to get their help. A German representative of the organisation, Bishop Helmut Frenz, took his request to the Ministry of Justice. He was asked to wait.

Just after midnight on 18 October the German Minister of State Wischnewski reported from Mogadishu to Bonn: 'The job's done.'

In Bonn, the representative of Amnesty International was still waiting. A senior official finally saw him after midnight.

The bishop made his request on behalf of Baader's lawyer, and the official is reported to have said that they could talk about it later that day, if it was still necessary. Some seven hours later all four terrorists would be found in their cells either dead or dying.

Jan-Karl Raspe was supposed to have used a 9mm Heckler and Koch pistol which he had hidden in the skirting board of his cell. He had put the gun to the right side of his head and fired. No shot was heard. Did he use some form of padding to deaden the sound? If so, I can find no mention or evidence of it.

Andreas Baader had hidden his 7.65 FEG gun in his record player in his cell; previously it had been hidden in his cell wall. He is said to have shot himself through the back of the neck after shooting two rounds into the wall, to make it look as if a struggle had taken place. Reports also say that he used a mattress to deaden the noise of the gun shots. I find it very difficult to believe that he could have knelt face down on the floor, put a mattress over the back of his head, then put the pistol against the mattress and pulled the trigger.

Gudrun Ensslin had hanged herself with a piece of towelling. She had tied the makeshift rope to the grating of her window and stood on a chair, which she then kicked away. It was a carbon copy of the death of her old friend Ulrike Meinhof. Irmgard Moller had taken a knife belonging to the prison cutlery and stabbed herself in the chest.

I have thought long and hard about these suicides and each time I come back to the same points – the two hand guns. I can accept that Gudrun Ensslin hanged herself. I can accept that Irmgard Moller stabbed herself. But I cannot accept the guns.

In the middle of the night, even in padded rooms, half the prison would have heard the shots – unless a silencer was used. Was one found? Was any test carried out using the same weapons under the same conditions to ascertain noise level?

But my overriding reason for having some doubt comes partly from what the German government would have us believe – that they all had some means of communicating from cell to cell, and that the suicides were carried out as a final act of vengeance in order to implicate the government. From the outset of Schleyer's kidnapping, all contact with the prisoners had been severed. According to official reports, apart from the guards only the two chaplains spoke to Ensslin while Minister Hegelau and Alfred Klaus spoke to Baader. The cells were searched on a regular basis and the four were moved from cell to cell while in-depth searches were carried out – nothing was found. Yet immediately after the suicides all the hiding places suddenly came to light.

My big question is this. Why, if they had guns with several rounds of ammunition, and they could talk to each other, did they not try to escape? Baader and Raspe's whole history as terrorists is one of shoot-outs with the police – never surrender. Ulrike Meinhof was a writer, a woman of words, but left no suicide note. Additionally, there are reports that forensic experts were forbidden by the police to enter the room and start their investigations. The reason given for this delay was that the police were waiting for international representatives so that they could establish fair play. All the delay achieved was to make it impossible to ascertain the precise time of death.

That said, when I consider the number of people who died violent deaths in the various rescue attempts, in order to free the Baader-Meinhof, I have to ask myself if society could have afforded the luxury of keeping them alive. It's us or them.

16

THE FINAL VICTIM

At around 1pm on 18 October both aircraft – containing rescuers and rescued – touched down at Frankfurt, where a massive reception had been laid on for the passengers. All the GSG9 and ourselves were asked to remain on board our 707. As we sat there, I saw a catering truck pull up and start to unload what I hoped was food. Wrong – it was just more alcohol!

I watched through the aircraft window as the passengers of LH181 finally made their original destination. There to greet them was a large reception committee of officials and photographers, while in the background a brass band played. As the tired passengers came down the steps, stewardesses rushed forward with bunches of roses. Suddenly we heard a huge sound of applause as stewardess Gaby Dillmann stepped down from the plane, supported by her fiancé. Much of the rejoicing was nevertheless overshadowed by the death of the pilot, Captain Jürgen Schumann, whose widow was present at the reception.

Some thirty minutes later we took off again for Bonn, where we were told a reception awaited for the conquering heroes, the GSG9. The moment we were airborne the liquid celebrations started once more. At about 3pm our aircraft landed in Bonn and I was amazed to see the lengths that the German government had gone to. Our plane taxied very close to the terminal buildings. There were brass bands playing, TV cameras everywhere, and a heavy presence of armed guards on top of the airport building. We sat there in anticipation. Then the door at the front of the aircraft opened and Ulrich Wegener and Minister Wischnewski went forward to meet the German top brass. As Wischnewski talked to the politicians, two very senior military-looking types in long overcoats came to speak to Wegener. There was a brief discussion. The senior officers instructed Wegener that his men should get out their now tattered uniforms, put them on and exit the aircraft smartly. He told me later that what he said in reply was, 'We fought like this, we go out like this.' There is no doubt that Wegener felt very much the man of the moment, and quite justifiably so. So he led his men off in civilian clothes, thanking us as we passed him going down the gangway.

The band played, the crowd cheered and speeches of glory were proclaimed. To tell you the truth Alastair and I were rather overwhelmed by all this – SAS men just do the job and sneak back to Britain. Then one day about a year later someone discreetly pins a medal on you – if you're lucky. The German minister who had been doing all the talking exchanged a few words with me. I said in English, 'Any time we can help, just give us a call.' I think all the alcohol I had drunk was making me a bit light-headed, because the next moment this minister was hugging me and telling me how wonderful I was.

Luckily I was saved by a man in a very long trenchcoat who whispered in my ear, 'Com wid me, I hav my orders.' Now when a German in a very long trenchcoat requests such a thing, you do as you're told. Alastair and I followed him through the crowd, leaving the parade behind, and were shown into the VIP lounge. Here, still dressed like tramps and stinking to high heaven, Alastair and I were greeted by slaps on the back and handshakes from Germany's industrial élite. For some reason they were all sitting there watching the welcome home parade on TV, when all they had to do was stand up and look out of the window!

The next moment yet another trolley full of drink arrived in front of us. Then, just before I had a chance to put my latest large gin and tonic to my lips, we were approached by two very smart gentlemen, who introduced themselves as senior representatives of Lufthansa and British Airways. Was there anything we needed they enquired of Alastair and me. If so, these two ladies would see to our every need. The two ladies in question had appeared with them, and were the most stunning stewardesses I have ever seen – one from Lufthansa and one from British Airways.

Alastair and I looked at each other and, then in all innocence, enquired if it was possible to have a shower and a shave.

'I'll go for Lufthansa,' I whispered out of the side of my mouth. I adopted my best macho stance. My luck seemed to be in again – to the heroes the spoils.

Then, suddenly, the German in the very long trenchcoat reappeared. 'Gentlemen, you have to stay as you are. Your government has requested your immediate return to Britain.'

Sadly, it was true. Dejectedly, Alastair and I followed the trenchcoat through the airport to the British Airways lounge. We sat there waiting for the next flight home, dreaming about what might have been. And, of course, we were informed that the flight to London was delayed . . .

To alleviate our boredom, one of the Lufthansa officials brought in the drinks trolley. It was quite amusing to watch the faces of all the other passengers booked on the London flight as they saw two scruffy, smelly individuals get the five-star treatment.

Later that evening we eventually arrived back in London. The moment the aircraft came to a halt, our names were called out and again bemused passengers watched as we got into a Ministry of Defence car. It took us to a debriefing in central London, where we were met at the door by the SAS Brigadier Johnny Watts, a man who never shirked danger despite his rank and status. As Alastair and I stood before him in the hallway he did not seem very pleased. 'Well, you're back. Where's the ransom money?' As if we would. Then he smiled and produced a bottle of champagne from behind his back. As I said, he's a good SAS soldier.

We were then shown into a private room containing half a dozen people and were just in time to watch the whole event on *News at Ten*. After this the questions came thick and furious, with Alastair and me trying hard to remember all the details.

Sometime during the debrief I fell into a deep sleep, brought on partly from lack of sleep and partly by too much alcohol. They kindly put me to bed, and apparently I kept everyone awake with my snoring.

Soon enough, thank God, I returned to normality. I travelled back to Hereford by train, arriving about 6pm. Quickly going into camp I retrieved my car, and since there was no one around I made my way home. Within the hour I had lit a welcoming fire and poured myself a drink; my little black and white cottage felt warm and comfortable. As it was still early, I decided to write an account of all the events while they were still fresh in my head. While I was doing this a friend, also on the anti-terrorist team, turned up. Over a few drinks I retold the story, still making notes.

'Have you kept any souvenirs?' he enquired.

'Yeah, one or two.' I reached for my bag and opened it.

'What's that evil smell?'

'Oh, sorry – it's my dirty washing from two weeks ago!' It was good to be home.

But the events at Mogadishu did not result in tearful reunions and pleasant homecomings for everyone. Many had been saved, but one would have to be sacrificed – for the family of Hans-Martin Schleyer, the news of the successful rescue and the Baader-Meinhof suicides would have done little to encourage their hopes of his safe return.

Justice Minister Hans-Jochen Vogel drove under heavy guard to the Schleyer home on the afternoon of 18 October. He tried to explain the government's position and to justify their actions at Mogadishu. He also told the family that the search for Schleyer would continue with renewed vigour, but at the same time he prepared them for the worst – as if they had not realised that the death sentence must now be a certainty.

Next day the family's worst fears were confirmed when the Bonn government telephoned to say that a French newspaper, *Libération*, had had a letter from the Siegfried Hausner Commando, saying that they had killed Schleyer. The body was stated to be in a green Audi parked in the Rue Charles Péguy in Mulhouse in eastern France. At 5pm the local police found the car. All the surrounding streets were closed off and at first no one was allowed near the vehicle in case it was booby-trapped. Some three hours later the car was safely opened, and inside the trunk they found the body of Hans-Martin Schleyer. All that the police would say was that his face looked distorted and that his hair had been cut short.

The autopsy, which was carried out by the French authorities, revealed that he had been shot in the head three times at very close range. Grass was found in his mouth and pine needles still clung to his clothing, indicating that he had possibly been shot in a forest before being dumped in the car. The Baader-Meinhof had claimed their last victim.

17

AT THE END OF THE DAY

The Israeli Prime Minister, Menachem Begin, and the Foreign Minister, Moshe Dayan, both sent messages of congratulations to the German Chancellor, Herr Schmidt, and the Minister of State, Herr Wischnewski, expressing their appreciation of the rescue of the Lufthansa hostages in Somalia. The Israelis compared the commando raid carried out so far from German soil with their own operation at Entebbe in July 1976.

Sometime between the Mogadishu incident and the Iranian Embassy siege in 1980 there was a meeting in Germany of all the anti-terrorist teams of the Western world. Britain and America had not had the opportunity to show their colours by then, so it was down to the Germans and the Israelis, who dominated the proceedings like long-lost brothers. I thought this was ironical, given that an Israeli could well have cocked up the whole Mogadishu assault.

In October 1977 an Israeli freelance journalist monitoring the skyways had picked up the fact that a Lufthansa aircraft carrying troops was on its way to Mogadishu. Correctly interpreting the dialogue between the aircraft and control tower, he guessed that there was to be an assault on the aircraft. The story went out on Israeli television and was picked up by the news services of other countries. The mayor of Jerusalem, Teddy Kollek, voiced a strong protest against Israeli television for broadcasting the news of an impending German rescue attempt several hours before it took place. Had the terrorists heard the news aboard LH181, the outcome might have been disastrous.

Due to the traumatic events of the hijack all scheduled visits to West Germany by heads of state had been cancelled; now they could resume. James Callaghan, the British Prime Minister, who was set to meet Chancellor Schmidt on one of their twice-yearly meetings, now found himself being warmly welcomed.

The main issue had been to get a tangible result on the signing of a new 'offset' agreement between the two countries, whereby Germany promised to pay £112,750,000 towards the foreign exchange costs of keeping the British Army in Germany. At the outset the West German government had been very reluctant to engage further in such commitments, and negotiations had been difficult. But after the Mogadishu success the pact was signed without further question by Sir Oliver Wright, the British Ambassador, and Herr Peter Hermes, German Secretary of State, in the Bonn Foreign Ministry.

One of the major lessons learnt through the Mogadishu episode was how well organised and co-ordinated the terrorists had become. In the early 1970s, while the governments of the Western world were only just beginning to prepare themselves to deal with hijacks and hostage-taking, the various terrorist groups were already training together. This is true not just in the case of the Baader-Meinhof and the PFLP, but also in connection with the Japanese Red Army, who carried out the Lod Airport shootings on behalf of the PFLP.

By the time of the Entebbe hijack it was clear that the

terrorists had the upper hand. For now they had enlisted not just another group to help them, but another country. It seemed almost impossible that anyone could rescue the Israeli hostages from Uganda, but they did. Then, during the Mogadishu hijack, the terrorist leader Mahmud never gave a single inch. He refused to release any hostage, no matter how sick. Moreover he was prepared to kill, and much worse he was prepared to die himself, taking the hostages with him.

But the thing that amazes me most of all is the co-ordination of the Schleyer kidnapping and the Mogadishu hijack, spelt out in detail in the letter sent to *The Times* which arrived just as the hostages had been released. Despite its windy rhetoric – it is printed in full on pp. 148–52 – the closely interwoven relationships between the terrorist groups are frighteningly clear.

Sometime after the Mogadishu affair the Germans held a big presentation for the GSG9 and the Lufthansa aircrew, at which the various medals and awards were handed over by Chancellor Helmut Schmidt himself. There was a very strong rumour at the time that two medals were presented in our absence to Alastair and myself. Questions were even asked in the national newspapers. The British Medals Office did not think it fitting that we should be awarded German 'Iron Crosses', as one paper put it. However, since that time the Medals Office has lost its Colonel Blimp image and has changed its policy.

Not long ago Alastair and I discussed all this. If the medals are still lying about gathering dust, somewhere in Germany, we would be delighted to receive them. But we cannot complain, for a little later the Germans held a private presentation for the both of us.

It was after I had finished my five-month tour with the anti-terrorist team, and my squadron was preparing itself to return to the Oman War in the Middle East. As part of my personal preparation I decided to attend a three-week refresher course at Oxford General Hospital to brush up on my medical skills and training.

As with all SAS hospital attachments, the staff were excellent and, providing one gets on with the doctors and nurses, and works equally hard, it can be a very pleasant and instructive time. During my second week I received a telephone call from HQ SAS, informing me that the Colonel, Alastair and I had been invited to the German Embassy for lunch, along with the British Defence Secretary. It would seem that the German government wanted to make a special presentation to Alastair and me.

On the day in question, as I was enjoying a glass of Germany's premium white wine, one of the Germans happened to mention some some snippet of information about my place of birth. Intrigued, I enquired as to how he had come by this information, only to be told that he had read my file.

'My file.' Staying cool, as if it was normal for allies to keep data on soldiers of other friendly countries, I asked politely if I could see 'my file'. But of course, no problem, the young German replied happily, and disappeared for a few moments, returning with a buff-coloured folder. Still smiling, he presented the inch-thick folder to me.

Now I was positively fascinated. What surprised me most of all was the photo of myself on the front. I recognised it instantly. The photograph had been taken in France on the 2 September 1974, three years earlier. At that time I was climbing in the Mount Blanc area, working with the French border police. The photograph had been taken for identity card purposes and clearly showed the pullover of the French border police that I had been wearing. Strange carry-on I thought.

We then sat down to a marvellous lunch. As it progressed the middle-aged Ambassador enquired what I would be doing next. I explained the SAS rota system to him, and the resultant benefits it produced, and said that for the next five months I would be involved in the Oman War. By this time we had finished eating and were well into the wine-drinking phase. The Ambassador was a very likeable man and he started to tell me a little about his own earlier military life.

In January 1943, when he was in his early twenties, he was fighting on the Russian Front. His Panzer battalion were fighting for their very existence as the Russian army pushed them back from the gates of Moscow. In some nameless village his battalion had been ordered to fight to the last man, and that moment was not far away. Totally surrounded, the young tank captain continued to operate, providing what little support he could give to the retreating German infantry. Suddenly he felt a massive jolt and his tank shuddered under the blast of high explosives. He knew that they had been badly hit.

As he sat there, dazed and shell-shocked, the hatch to his tank was thrown open and there looking down at him stood a Russian soldier. Helplessly, the young captain watched as, with a sneer on his face, the Russian thrust his machine gun down into the tank, pointing it a few inches from his head.

'The last thing I remember seeing was this dirty finger pulling the trigger. I will never forget it – the nail was all cracked and broken and thick with dirt. Then, as I waited for death, there was a *clunk* as the breach of the Russian's gun fell on an empty magazine. I knew then that this was not my moment to die, so I pulled out my pistol and shot the surprised Russian. Minutes later I was making good my escape.'

As the Ambassador told this story, the light of youth drifted back into his eyes.

After lunch, Alastair and I were presented with silver cigarette boxes and a framed photograph of Helmut Schmidt. The cigarette boxes, like all presentations to the Regiment, went to the SAS mess, but we were allowed to keep the photographs as they had been personally signed for us. The Chancellor had sent a personal message, which was read out during the presentation:

> Dear Secretary of State, Gentlemen!
>
> It is with deep gratitude and pride that I present to Major Morrison and Staff Sergeant Davies these personal gifts of the Chancellor of the Federal Republic of Germany, Herr Helmut Schmidt.
>
> They are not rewards, because what you, Major Morrison and Staff Sergeant Davies, have done cannot be rewarded by presents. But they are a little token of appreciation for your courageous deed in Mogadishu.
>
> You have risked your own lives to save the lives of innocent men, women and children – and your brave act has an importance even beyond that:
>
> It constitutes a further decisive step in our common struggle against international terrorism and it proves that our societies and our nations – as vulnerable as they may be – are not totally defenceless.
>
> Mogadishu, similar to Entebbe, is a symbol of hope for all of us who are threatened by international terrorism and it gives new confidence to our peoples who have seen how closely and successfully our two governments co-operate.
>
> Not only the Federal Chancellor and the Government of the Federal Republic of Germany, but the whole German people are deeply grateful to you.

Hans-Martin Schleyer was buried in his home town of Stuttgart on 25 October. The service, a small family affair, was held at the Collegiate Church. Government ministers were asked not to attend apart from President Scheel, who said to the family, 'In the name of all German citizens, I ask you, the family of Hans-Martin Schleyer, for forgiveness.'

Captain Jürgen Schumann, the pilot of LH181 who was shot by the hijackers in Aden, was buried in his home town of Badenhausen near Darmstadt. I must go there one day.

Andreas Baader, Jan-Karl Raspe and Gudrun Ensslin were all buried in a communal grave in the public cemetery in Stuttgart. According to the newspapers it was their final wish. I remember the funeral well – television stations around the world showed the service at the cemetery live. There were over a thousand armed police there, as well as a lot of Baader-Meinhof supporters carrying placards proclaiming: 'The Fight Goes On'.

It did. For six days between 30 April and 5 May 1980 six armed terrorists took over the Iranian Embassy at Princes Gate in London. This time the beast was ready – but that's another story.